America's RAIL *Pictorial*

By Russ Porter

Dedication

To my two children, Bob and Sue,
and to my wife of 54 years, Florence,
who went on our first date to watch
the *Hiawatha* rush by in a cloud of dust.

Library of Congress Catalog Card Number: 97-72338
ISBN: 0-911581-42-1
First Edition
Printed in Hong Kong

HEIMBURGER HOUSE PUBLISHING COMPANY
7236 West Madison Street
Forest Park, Illinois 60130

Contents

Foreword....................................4

Atchison, Topeka & Santa Fe...................6

Baltimore & Ohio..........................10

Chicago, Burlington & Quincy.....................13

Chicago & Eastern Illinois....................26

Chesapeake & Ohio.......................27

Chicago Short Line........................31

Chicago Great Western....................32

Canadian National........................34

Canadian Pacific..........................38

Chicago & Western Indiana...............42

Duluth, Missabe & Iron Range............43

Duluth & Northeastern....................48

Duluth, Winnipeg & Pacific..............52

Elgin, Joliet & Eastern.....................54

Erie-Lackawanna...........................57

Green Bay & Western.....................61

Gulf, Mobile & Ohio.......................67

Great Northern............................71

Grand Trunk Western.....................76

Greater Winnipeg Water District Railway.....................82

Illinois Central.........................83

Lake Superior & Ishpeming...................88

Manufacturers Railway of St. Louis.............92

Minneapolis, Northfield & Southern...........93

Monon.....................................95

Nickel Plate Road.........................96

New York Central........................100

Norfolk & Western.......................104

Northern Pacific.........................106

Northwestern Steel & Wire...............115

Pennsylvania.............................116

Rock Island..............................124

Soo Line.................................132

Terminal Railroad Association...............143

Toledo, Peoria & Western................144

Union Pacific............................146

Wabash..................................150

Foreword

A Soo freight is about to cross the Milwaukee Road tracks at DuPlainville, Wisconsin.

Growing up in Chicago, the Railroad hub of America, had its advantages. Living first in the northwest suburb of Austin, and later in Elmwood Park, I had easy access via street car to the downtown Chicago railroad passenger stations.

On such trips, I spent hours at any one of the stations viewing such famous trains as Chicago & NorthWestern's *400* fleet, Burlington's *Exposition Flyer* and *Zephyrs*, Grand Trunk Western's *Maple Leaf*, Illinois Central's *City of New Orleans*, Milwaukee Road's *Hiawatha*, New York Central's *20th Century Limited*, Pennsy's *Broadway Limited* and Santa Fe's *Super Chief*.

In the mid-1920s my parents had friends living on a farm south of LaGrange, Illinois. We visited them frequently, and my dad, not trusting our Model T's tires, would often take us there by way of the West Towns street car, which ended its run alongside the Burlington depot in LaGrange. There his friend was waiting for us with his horse and buggy. I recall that the buggy had side curtains and a fringed top and came with heavy wool blankets to keep us warm. Many years later, the Electro-Motive diesel plant was built just across the road from that farm. We usually spent a few days at the farm and then were taken back to the depot, where we caught the suburban steam train back to Chicago. Headend power was a reliable 4-6-2 Pacific, followed by a number of open end coaches. The crew often fought a losing battle keeping the steps clear of blowing snow. A cold blast of air would enter the car at every stop. And so it was not too pleasant a trip.

The 1933-34 World's Fair at Chicago's lakefront did much to increase my interest in railroads. Outside the Transportation Building, I was able to walk through and compare the English steam powered *Royal Scot* with the Burlington composite train made of equipment from regular trains headed by a Class 0-5 4-8-4 Northern steam locomotive. Inside the building were many fascinating exhibits including an O gauge scale operating model railroad. This railroad was later installed (I believe) in Chicago's Museum of Science & Industry. Today that railroad has unfortunately been modernized with up-to-date diesels and runs without cabooses.

We had relatives in the East, and during summer vacation in the 30s the family traveled via the *Broadway Limited* to Philadelphia. I marveled that Pullman Porter George (no relation) always remembered my dad's name from previous trips and how he handled the wiskbroom so deftly on dad and me at the end of the trip. Shortly after boarding the train, I would rush to the open observation platform, get comfortable on one of the chairs and watch the scenery go by. Just outside Englewood Station on the south side of Chicago our train occasionally raced New York Central's crack *20th Century Limited*, which paralleled our tracks for a considerable distance. On a weekly basis, I would have to say, the races ended in a tie. A few hours after dusk, George would come out to the platform and take this soot-covered urchin back to my dismayed parents.

After visiting in Philadelphia, we would travel to Wilmington, Delaware via a Pennsy train powered by a

A maroon and yellow Rock Island Geep hauls coal loads at a power plant in LaSalle, Illinois.

Alco-GE 1,000 hp RS-1 #254 awaits a clear signal on the Chicago & Western Indiana at 21st Street crossing in Chicago.

GG-1. There we transferred to a train destined for the ocean resort town of Rehoboth Beach, Delaware. I don't recall where we changed from electric to steam power, but I can remember listening to the stack music of the locomotive as it pulled up Main Street at Rehoboth Beach and stopped at the small depot, located just a block or two from the ocean boardwalk. My grandparents owned a restaurant there, so working in the kitchen during the summer vacation period I acquired a taste for seafood, which has stayed with me to this day.

GOT BOX CAMERA AS GIFT

Grandmother gave me a Kodak box camera as a birthday gift in the early 1930s and that started my picture-taking days. When not taking pictures at the downtown stations, I headed for Englewood Station where trains came and went constantly: Nickel Plate, New York Central, Pennsy and Rock Island. Unfortunately, the days I picked were usually foggy, rainy or overcast. Needless to say the photos were unforgiving. Later on, equipped with a Kodak Vigilant #620 folding camera, much better results were obtained.

In 1937, I made a round trip between Chicago and Milwaukee on board a *Hiawatha*. At Milwaukee I raced to the west end of the depot and managed to photograph two of the steam *Hiawatha* "A's" side by side. A beautiful sight.

When the Vigilant #620 developed a bellows leak, I turned to a Kodak Retina, and later an Argus C-3. With an ASA 10 rating, color was used sparingly until the entrance of the early, colorful diesels. Then I switched to color almost 100%. Oh to have had the new cameras and the film back in the days when so much steam and early diesels were available!

CHICAGO RAILROADS

As you page through this book you will notice the majority of them show railroads that radiated from downtown Chicago. Ideal places to watch the many trains were: Roosevelt Road viaduct overlooking Grand Central and Dearborn St. stations, the south end of Union Station, Illinois Central Station, 21 St. crossing, Englewood Station, Joliet Union Station and Griffith, Indiana.

Knowing the end of steam was near in the late 50s, my wife, two kids and I planned our vacation trips to cover the last strongholds of steam. Thus the Nickel Plate Berkshires at Calumet Yard, Illinois were aptly covered, as was the activity on the Grand Trunk Western at Durand, Michigan and Canadian National steam and diesels at Windsor, Canada. Other trips took us to see steam and early diesels at the Twin Cities; Grand Island, Nebraska; Marquette, Michigan; Proctor, Minnesota; Cloquet, Minnesota; and Winnipeg, Canada.

I hope you enjoy the photos in this book as much as I did taking them, although some were taken in less than ideal conditions such as the camera inside my coat to keep the shutter from freezing, or from getting wet in a downpour. Then, mosquitoes always seemed to gather in hordes while the camera was on the tripod for a very long night exposure. Strange, though, after the photo was developed and looked good, all the irritating problems were forgotten.

Looking back on 66 years of picture taking, I do have some unforgettable memories: a Pennsy GG-1 at Wilmington, Delaware; three GTW steamers at the Durand, Michigan crossing; a DM&IR 2-8-8-4 battling the grade out of Proctor, Minnesota; a gathering of Berkshires at the coaling tower at Calumet, Illinois; and a Monon BL-2 hurrying its train along at Calumet, Illinois. *Russ Porter*

Atchison, Topeka & Santa Fe

ABOVE. At Joliet, Illinois in May, 1970, the Warbonnet paint scheme, applied to the Santa Fe F-7A diesel passenger units, was a delight to behold. A year later, Amtrak took over the nation's passenger service.

LEFT. Facing the fading sun, Santa Fe FT units await assignment at Chicago's Corwith Yard in June, 1960. The FM switcher in the background has finished its chores for the day.

Blowing snow shrouds, a westbound trailer train approaches the Indiana Harbor Belt Railway crossing at McCook, Illinois. The walkway atop the semaphore bridge is not the ideal place to photograph trains in weather like this. Date: January, 1971.

Just minutes away from Chicago's Dearborn Station in January, 1968, the *Texas Chief* clatters across the Pennsy diamond at 21st Street. The lead unit is a rare GE U30CG, one of only six built for the Santa Fe.

San Francisco Chief

New train   between San Francisco and Chicago
with thru service to Houston
and New Orleans

The last of 10 units built for the Santa Fe, U28CG #359 powers the *Grand Canyon* away from Chicago's Dearborn Station in November of 1968.

With plenty of headend power, the *Chief* passes 21st Street tower in May of 1971 on its westward journey to Los Angeles. Photographers on the side are awaiting a Grand Trunk Western steam-powered excursion train whose smoke appears above the lead diesel unit.

In August, 1960, Alco RS-1 #2395 switcher, equipped with a steam boiler for heating passenger cars, prepares to move a passenger train from Chicago's Dearborn Street Station to the coach yard. There the cars will be cleaned and refurbished, and then be returned to the station.

Under dark and threatening skies, Santa Fe #17, the *Super Chief*, glides out of Dearborn Street Station, Chicago on December, 1936. Famous box cab diesels #1 and 1A built by General Motors and the St. Louis Car Company in late 1935 had a combined 3,600 hp. In 1938 #1 was altered with a higher nose to protect the crew in the event of a grade crossing accident.

B&O

ABOVE. Just minutes away from the Saginaw, Michigan yard, a local freight, headed by GP-40-2 #4209, rushes westward. With the crossing gate coming down with little warning and no chance to get out of the car, this photo was taken from the passenger side of the car in September of 1985.

LEFT. A noon time sun beams down on two competitors at the B&O Robey Street roundhouse area, near downtown Chicago in June of 1957. A very clean Alco FA-2 #4021 has just come in from a freight run. EMD #9511 switcher crew is taking a lunch break in the roundhouse.

Mountain type 4-8-2 #718 rests quietly in the Robey Street roundhouse, Chicago, on April 5, 1959. Its long service career has come to an end, and the scrap yard is not far away.

Flanked on the right by refrigerator cars ready for a Chicago packing plant and on the left by the nearly-filled Santa Fe coach yard, a Santa Fe passenger train gets the green light for the 21st Street diamond in October of 1968. Bringing up the rear, on a special move, is a classic B&O solarium lounge car.

In a one of a kind appearance, a B&O Shriners Special passenger train stops at the Milwaukee Road depot at Milwaukee in September of 1955. *Hiawatha* skytop lounge-bedroom car *Spanish Creek* makes a striking contrast to the 1930s dignified heavyweight B&O solarium lounge car.

On a cold morning in February of 1967 Chicago's Central Station sees some activity. After the Soo Line abandoned passenger service to the station, a C&O switcher was assigned switching duties. Here switcher #5115 pushes in some cars, while on an adjoining track, two B&O E units move in to couple onto their train.

Far from home, a series of B&O Geeps southbound with #3511 leading, pass a track maintenance crew at Wisconsin Dells, Wisconsin in February of 1978. The depot was destroyed on July 4, 1982 in a coal train wreck.

Chicago, Burlington & Quincy

An unusual sight in the last days of steam—a freshly-painted CB&Q Mikado 2-8-2 freight locomotive makes a beautiful sight at Savanna, Illinois in 1958 as it does what a steam locomotive does best—belch smoke and steam.

Two CB&Q F-3s and two FTs make up the power for Extra 124D on the eastbound holding track at Eola, Illinois in October of 1956. With the main line in use, 124D must await a green light before proceeding to Chicago.

In 1929, the Whitcomb Locomotive Company furnished 44 ton switchers No. 9100 through 9120 to the CB&Q. Here at Millington, Illinois the #9120 rests quietly on a siding during a weekend in October of 1956.

In a rare downtown La Crosse, Wisconsin street running scene, CB&Q 4-8-4 #5632 moves cautiously through traffic on a fantrip special from Chicago in July of 1959.

Enroute to Ottawa, Illinois CB&Q 2-8-2 #4960 makes a splendid winter scene as it moves through Sheridan, Illinois in December of 1950. Smoke and steam obscure the passenger cars of this fantrip special.

Locomotive #5631 moves up the service track to take on water and coal at Savanna, Illinois on a 1958 CB&Q fantrip special. Then it will be turned for the trip back to Chicago.

CB&Q E-8 passenger diesel #9945B built in 1955 by EMD awaits assignment at the Minneapolis yard in May of 1955. The ornamental protective covers for the coupler will soon be discarded for more efficient maintenance.

ABOVE. CB&Q 2-8-2 #4960 roars past the Millington, Illinois depot on December 28, 1958 during a photo runby for fans, who had alighted earlier to set up cameras and tripods. This was one of many steam fantrips of the late '50s and early '60s that had the cooperation of CB&Q management.

LEFT. On the high speed three-track main line just east of Naperville, Illinois in November of 1958, an eastbound CB&Q freight leans into a gentle curve, as the conductor waves a friendly greeting. A colorful Chicago & North Western green and yellow stock car proceeds the caboose.

With steam becoming scarce in 1956, CB&Q 4-8-4 #5615 was a welcome sight despite its shabby appearance. Here at Eola, Illinois it moves eastward past the extensive yard on the left, an important interchange location with the EJ&E.

The graceful lines of a thoroughbred are apparent in this side view of CB&Q 4-8-4 #5631 at Savanna, Illinois in 1958. When the steam era ended, #5631 was donated for display at Sheridan, Wyoming.

PREVIOUS PAGE TOP. While two nearly new units headed by GP-30 #954 go through the wash racks, a brakeman sets the turnout for GP-7 #247 to enter the locomotive servicing area at Galesburg, Illinois in September of 1963.

PREVIOUS PAGE BOTTOM. CB&Q 4-6-4 #3001 prepares to make a photo runby during a fantrip to Rock Island, Illinois in September of 1958. The baggage car on this trip was most welcome as it carried soda and snacks. Locomotive #3001 was donated for display at Ottumwa, Iowa.

ABOVE. This could be a turn of the century glance at an old CB&Q steam locomotive. However, it is a November 1962 look at a portion of 4-6-0 #637, showing through a side door of the roundhouse at Eola, Illinois. The locomotive used for historical exhibits along the CB&Q was donated to Aurora, Illinois for display.

CB&Q 2-8-2 #4960 had the honor of being the first steam locomotive in modern times to power the circus train from Baraboo, Wisconsin to Milwaukee in July of 1965. Here at Circus City, the engineer carefully backs the veteran steamer, complete with auxiliary water tender, toward the consist of colorful wagons and coaches filled with circus fans.

CB&Q's 4-8-4 #5632 slowly passes the northbound *Empire Builder,* which has just stopped at the Savanna, Illinois depot. It is a cold, damp, dreary day in March, 1962 as the fantrip steamer emits dense clouds of smoke and steam, much to the delight of the hardy photographers nearby.

Burlington Route

A CB&Q steam-powered freight train in 1962? Looks authentic enough, but it is actually a mixed freight-passenger fantrip out of Chicago. Locomotive #5632, a 4-8-4, is rolling along at 50 mph as it comes westward out of the curve at Hinckley, Illinois on June 23, 1962.

The December, 1962 northbound *Morning Zephyr* stops briefly at the East Dubuque, Illinois depot before continuing its journey to the Twin Cities. Most of the way will be along the picturesque Mississippi River shown to the left of the train. In the upper right is the Illinois Central bridge, which links East Dubuque, Illinois with downtown Dubuque, Iowa.

CB&Q freight with SD-24 #510 leading, rushes westward near Zearing, Illinois in April of 1960. The level Illinois countryside offers little resistance for the 2,400 hp #510 and her helpers.

CB&Q SD-9 #365 brings a cut of cars out of the shadows in December of 1969 to the freight interchange track at Prairie Du Chien, Wisconsin. The brakeman is about to step off to line up the turnout. The main line tracks are to the left of the modern looking depot.

The westbound *Nebraska Zephyr* hits its stride on the high speed middle track at West Hinsdale, Illinois in May of 1968. In the distance the headlight of a local commuter train can be seen. The shelter at the left gave protection from the weather for many commuters.

Eastbound CB&Q #9217 NW-2 1,000 hp EMD switcher built in May 1941, brings a short freight out of the Illinois Central tunnel at East Dubuque, Illinois in December of 1967. The train, with trackage rights, has come from Dubuque, Iowa, crossed the Mississippi River bridge, crossed the CB&Q main and entered the tunnel, which curves to the right and is parallel to the CB&Q main. Shortly, the train will switch to the eastbound CB&Q main.

National Railroad Historical Society fantrip [lo]comotive #5632 emerges from the curved tunn[el] mentioned earlier, at East Dubuque, Illinois [in] September of 1961. The big Northern does[n't] have much clearance on either side, especial[ly] in a curved tunnel. Too, the engineer has to wo[rry] about automotive traffic in front of the tunnel [as] there are no crossing gates.

The *Morning Zephyr* speeds along the scenic hillsides of Wisconsin and curving Mississippi River in June of 1970 on its way to the Twin Cities. The short train is a far cry from the original, but at least it has three dome cars.

ABOVE. It's one of those days when commuters are glad they can depend on the train to get them to their Chicago jobs on time. Here an E unit bumped from through train service, comes to a stop at Western Springs, Illinois in February of 1971.

LEFT. EMD 1,000 hp #9213 switcher built in 1941 keeps busy in the CB&Q passenger car yard near downtown Chicago in May of 1968.

Making a rare appearance as a fantrip locomotive, CB&Q 4-8-4 #5618 waits with its train at the St. Paul, Minnesota depot for the return trip to Chicago in July of 1958. Even this locomotive did not escape the wrecker's torch.

Chicago & Eastern Illinois

Using Chicago & Western Indiana trackage, a Chicago & Eastern Illinois transfer run in May of 1968 approaches the 21st Street crossing.

EMD E-7 #1100 powers the eastbound *Danville Flyer*, C&EI's only passenger train to Chicago, across the Pennsy tracks at 21st Street in May of 1968.

C&EI GP-7 #93 brings a transfer freight to the 21st Street crossing in Chicago in May of 1968. With the railroad becoming part of the Missouri Pacific, the familiar red circle emblem soon disappeared and was replaced with the MP "buzz saw" emblem.

Chesapeake & Ohio

C&O GP-38 #3887 and GP-39 #3917 lead an eastbound freight at Griffith, Indiana, over the multiple crossings of Penn Central, Grand Trunk Western, Erie-Lackawanna and Elgin, Joliet & Eastern in October of 1971. With this many crossings, the man with the stop sign had plenty to do.

With snow covering the ground in February, 1967 C&O diesel switcher #5115 maneuvers a string of baggage cars into a loading track at Grand Central Station in Chicago.

A trio of C&O diesels led by GP-7 #5899 sends up a dense cloud of black smoke as the eastbound fast freight thunders by on Chicago's south side in April of 1971.

On a clear day in June 1971 at Jones Island in Milwaukee, C&O EMD 1,200 hp SW-9 #5251 starts to pull out the idler flat cars (used to balance the boat when loading freight cars) from the hold of the railroad car ferry *Spartan*. Spectators enjoyed this action every day until the railroad decided it was less expensive to reroute freight around Chicago instead of sending it via Ludington to Milwaukee and visa versa.

A 16-year-old Lima-built C&O #1613 Class H-8 2-6-6-6 Allegheny awaits its fate at a scrap yard in Gary, Indiana in 1957. These super locomotives were built during WWII. It was an awesome sight to see one of these brutes on the head end of a long coal train, assisted by a twin at the rear in West Virginia coal field territory.

Detroit to Chicago westbound C&O extra #7512 passes the unique Lake Odessa, Michigan depot which is almost dwarfed by the giant grain storage bins. It appears the siding track is little used in August of 1981 and will eventually disappear under the weeds.

Mershon Tower at Saginaw, Michigan in January of 1981 still had the old fashioned hand throw switch levers. More interesting was the track diagram. The hortizontal tracks from top to bottom were the Pere Marquette, Grand Trunk Western and C&O. The vertical track was C&O, which came from the yard, crossed or interchanged with the other railroads and continued west.

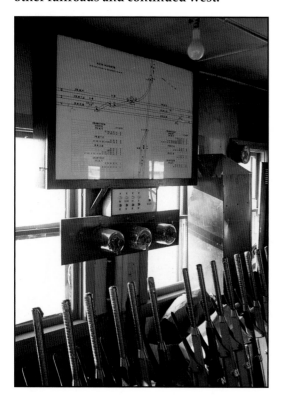

A pair of Alco C-630s 3,000 hp diesels #2100 and #2102, rush a fast freight westbound on the south edge of Chicago past an unusual signal tower in May of 1971. The front trackage is Penn Central.

In March of 1970, C&O Chicago to Muskegon, Michigan daily passenger train #8 arrives at Muskegon at 10:55 p.m. The one passenger car seems to foretell the upcoming abandonment of service.

Chicago Short Line

Heading for the B&O and Penn Central main line in 1971, Chicago Short Line switchers #30 and #25 ascend the steep grade from the railroad's main terminal on the southeast side of Chicago. The Chicago Short Line, a freight only road, provides switching and interchange services for industries and railroads on the southeast side of Chicago.

Chicago Short Line cabooses mingle with freight cars in the railroad's major yard, located near 95th Street and Avenue N in Chicago. The locomotive facility is located on the southeast side of the yard.

Chicago Short Line EMD switcher #27 moves a freight west at Pullman Junction, Illinois over Baltimore & Ohio Chicago Terminal track. This track connects with the Illinois Central at Bensenville.

Chicago Great Western

A Chicago Great Western freight powered with F units speeds eastward through Sycamore, Illinois in March of 1967. In July of 1968 the CGW was merged with the Chicago & NorthWestern.

TOP LEFT. In August of 1963, CGW 300 hp Winton-powered combine switcher #1000 sits on a siding at Winona, Minnesota. Doomed by a change in the full crew law, #1000 handled its last assignment in June of 1964. Hard to believe but this unit was once a McKeen flat-nosed gas-powered locomotive, express, baggage and railroad post office car of the *Bluebird*. The *Bluebird* was built in the railroad's shops at Oelwein, Iowa in 1929 and was advertised as the world's first streamlined train.

TOP RIGHT. This is another view of #1000 at Winona, Minnesota in August of 1963. When it was built in 1910, it had the familiar knife nose front end, which was replaced by a flat nose when it was rebuilt in 1929 to power the *Bluebird*. During the later part of 1964, it was sold to the Kettle Moraine Railway, a tourist line, at North Lake, Wisconsin.

CENTER. Alco switcher #1218 crosses a downtown street in Rochester, Minnesota in July of 1970. The SW-1200 1,200 hp unit surprisingly still retains its CGW colors and herald. This photo was taken in July of 1970.

A freshly painted caboose with an escorting diesel heads west on the CGW main line near St. Charles, Illinois in March, 1966. Since the C&NW merger, this section of the CGW was found to be unnecessary and was torn up.

Canadian National

An old enginehouse at Fort Rouge, Winnipeg, Canada, provides servicing and shelter for a Canadian National switcher and several F units in August of 1959.

BELOW. CN Vancouver-Montreal *Super Continental* eastbound with FP-9A #6519 1,750 hp leading stops at the Oba, Ontario, Canada station in October of 1970. It has just crossed the Algoma Central tracks, which run to Hearst and Sault Ste. Marie, Ontario. The Algoma Central train has come from Hearst and in a rare occurrence, has met the CN train, which was running late.

Looking the worst for wear in 1959, CN 2-8-2 #3599 moves up to the water tank at Transcona, Winnipeg. Many of the steam locomotives built at Transcona were brought back here for scrapping, and the #3599 was no exception.

In August of 1958, Pacific 4-6-4 #5701 awaits assignment at Windsor, Ontario, Canada. The side of the locomotive was illuminated by a yard tower light and the smokebox front by the headlight of a diesel sitting on the same track a few feet away.

Light Pacific 4-6-2 #5140 receives a drink of water at the Fort Rouge engine facility in 1959. Note the portion added to the tender when the locomotive was converted from coal to oil.

A number of CN diesels rest quietly between runs at the Fort Rouge enginehouse. Sporting the old but handsome color scheme and maple leaf emblem, F-7A diesel #9110, with headlight on, prepares to leave.

In Windsor, Ontario in 1958, side lighted by a yard tower light, CN 4-8-4 #6234 shows off its massive machinery of main and side rods. Lighting of the smokebox front would have been a problem except that the employee parking lot enabled parking the old Buick nearby, so that its bright lights illuminated the locomotive.

In the waning days of steam, even light Pacifics were used frequently in freight service. Here on a trip from Winnipeg to Portage La Prairie, Manitoba, Canadian National Pacific #5145 clouds a nearby highway with black smoke as it hurries its train along on a nearly perfect day in August of 1959.

Instead of a scene from the old steam days, this is CN 4-8-4 #6218 preparing to depart Chicago with a fantrip in November of 1966. A few seconds more, and the locomotive would have been hidden by the incoming Santa Fe diesels. On the far right, a Santa Fe switcher brings out some cars to the nearby 18th Street coach yard.

Canadian Pacific

With a slight drizzle falling, Canadian Pacific Montreal-Vancouver *Canadian* speeds westward in 1970 at Schreiber, Ontario. This train was CP's top scenic dome stainless steel streamliner.

While the engineer prepares to inspect his locomotive, the fireman pulls the valve to release water into the tender of CP 4-6-0 #930 at Portage La Prairie, Manitoba in 1959. The auxiliary water tender will be next, and then #930 will resume its wayfreight duties.

During a drizzling October rain, CP's *Canadian* comes into Terrace Bay, Ontario. The stop will be brief as only one passenger is ready to board.

ABOVE. Rain reflected ties add a somber view to the CP engine facility at White River, Ontario. Headlights on, some of the diesels will soon go out on trains to the east and west.

LEFT. CP baggage-combine *Dayliner* air conditioned RDC #9112 awaits passengers at Sault Ste. Marie in July of 1974. The *Dayliner* operated daily between Sault Saint Marie and Sudbury, Ontario, a distance of 179.3 miles.

Framed between two big grain elevators, CP #2343 streamer drifts eastward at Portage La Prairie, Manitoba in August of 1959. Unfortunately for the photographer, #2343 shows little if any smoke.

CP 2-8-2 #2425 with its tender full of coal above the top, awaits orders to take out a freight train from Webwood, Ontario in August, 1957.

Chicago & Western Indiana

ABOVE. Chicago & Western Indiana RS-1 1,000 hp Alco diesel switcher #259 in October of 1966 rests between two passenger cars at its terminal at Dearborn Street Station, Chicago. The car with the unusual roof design is a Stillwell coach, an ancient relic.

LEFT. C&WI Alco RS-1 1,000 hp diesel switchers are at the road's terminal at Dearborn Street Station in 1969. Main job of this railroad was to furnish switching service for the various railroads that used the station. At one time the railroad had considerable suburban passenger service, which dwindled to almost nothing in the '60s.

Duluth, Missabe & Iron Range

ABOVE. Duluth, Missabe & Iron Range Class M4, Baldwin-built (1943) 2-8-8-4 #231, drifts toward the yard at Proctor, Minnesota in August of 1959. Though begrimed, the big giant still shows its attractive green-colored boiler.

RIGHT. Massive DM&IR 2-8-8-4 #224 Class M3 built by Baldwin in 1941 is being prepared for service at Proctor. The locomotive had been recently shopped, as very little grime is in evidence in this July, 1961 scene.

Down the big hill to Duluth goes 2-10-2 #514 with water tank car and caboose in September of 1962. There #514 with tank car will be coupled to a fantrip special. Built by Alco in 1919, this massive locomotive was scrapped in 1962.

Just west of Proctor in October, 1955, DM&IR #237 2-8-8-4 uses full throttle as it pulls 150 empties toward the mines at Virginia, Minnesota. A little grimy, but still a wonderful machine to behold. It was the last of the M4 Yellowstones built in 1943 by Baldwin.

What a change from a few years earlier when this roundhouse at Proctor was filled with 2-8-8-4s in every stall. Now, in 1968 the stalls are empty of the steamers and a forlorn locomotive tender sits at left of the EMD road switchers. On the near track is the DM&IR business car *Northland*. Built in 1916 by Pullman, the car carried such distinguished guests as President Calvin Coolidge and his wife in 1928 and King Olaf of Norway and Queen in the 1930s. In 1978 the car was placed on the National Register of Historic Places.

ABOVE. Laying down a heavy, black screen of smoke over downtown Duluth in July of 1961, DM&IR 2-8-8-4 #225 moves out with a string of passenger cars, containing members of the Minnesota Railfans Association on a fantrip to the mines. The #225 was saved and put on display at Proctor.

RIGHT. Late at night, prior to the fantrip pictured above, #225 rests between the competition in the roundhouse at Proctor.

ABOVE. Fifteen months later #225 is seen in the Proctor roundhouse, but this time, with sister engine #226. What quirk of fate decided to scrap the #226 and save the #225?

LEFT. An unusual sight at the Proctor roundhouse area was the converted Duluth street car, used as an employee transportation car. It operated between Proctor and the roundhouse.

DM&IR 2-8-8-4 #231 moving along at about six miles an hour, is taking its load of ore cars over the weighing scales just on the outskirts of the Proctor classification yard in May of 1959.

After uncoupling from its load of heavy ore cars in spring of 1959, #231 runs light to the roundhouse service track. There it will be given coal and water and turned on the turntable in readiness for a trip back to the mines.

Duluth & Northeastern

ABOVE. Duluth & Northeastern 2-8-0 #14 switches cars at Cloquet, Minnesota on a cold, but sunny day in December of 1960. The veteran #14 was built by Baldwin in 1913. This shortline road was incorporated in 1898 and operated 75 miles of trackage between Cloquet and Hornby, Minnesota.

LEFT. This is a view from the caboose, as D&NE 2-8-0 #28 road engine (ex-DM&IR) switches on the wye at Saginaw, Minnesota. Cars for the DM&IR are set out and then picked up by the D&NE. The fare for riding the caboose in September of 1962 was 15¢ roundtrip. The 11.4 mile long railroad connected with the Burlington Northern at Cloquet and the DM&IR at Saginaw.

Sanding of locomotive flues can make for an interesting photo, and here the fireman in this July, 1957 shot does a magnificent job. Old 2-8-0 #16 built in 1913 by Baldwin was saved for display at Cloquet. Wonder what the EPA would have thought about this smoke job?

Not having a turntable, D&NE locomotives always faced the direction they were delivered to the railroad. Thus, we see two of them in July of 1961, posed as always, in the enginehouse at Cloquet.

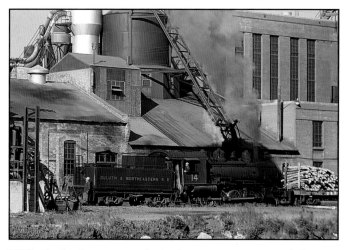

With the brakeman ready to throw a turnout, and the engineer cautiously backing #14, a load of pulpwood is being delivered to a customer at Cloquet in July of 1961.

D&NE 2-8-0 #28 works the wye in September of 1962 at Saginaw, Minnesota preparing to set out and pick up cars from the DM&IR. This train operated six days a week bringing out wood products to the DM&IR and receiving chemicals and supplies for the four paper mills it served.

In a classic scene from the past, D&NE 2-8-0 #14 comes upgrade working every inch of the way. The engineer keeps a sharp eye for traffic on the approaching highway near Saginaw in July of 1961. Maintenance on this locomotive left much to be desired, but then diesel power was soon to arrive.

D&NE 0-6-0 #29 backs away from the enginehouse at Cloquet, ready for a day's work at industries along the line. Unfortunately none of the engines operated with headlights during the day, thus the boiler front was dark. The tall building behind the locomotive was a grain elevator until the famous 1918 Cloquet fire destroyed the town, but the elevator and a few other buildings were saved. The railroad then converted the building into a coaling tower.

No D&NE tenders were alike. All locomotives are facing toward the enginehouse at Cloquet on this very hot day in July of 1960. The slope-backed tender belongs to 0-6-0 #30, the squat tender belongs to 0-6-0 #29, and the long distance tender belongs to 2-8-0 #28.

As the fireman guides the water tank spout into the innards of #14, the engineer checks the gauges. The track in front of the locomotive used to cross the river, but a flood in May of 1960 took out the bridge. A new main line bridge was built to the east where the river is narrow. Enough of the old main line remained to reach the water tank.

Duluth, Winnipeg & Pacific

Transporting a switch crew on its tender, Duluth, Winnipeg & Pacific 2-8-0 #1983 heads for the yard and work at Duluth in July of 1956. Influence of parent road Canadian National is seen in the locomotive design and color of the emblem on the tender. The DW&P ran from Fort Frances, Ontario, Canada to Duluth, Minnesota.

DW&P RDC-3 passenger, baggage-express-mail #301 pauses in August of 1959 at Orr, Minnesota on its 171.6 mile trip from Ft. Francis, Ontario. This was close to the end of passenger service on this line.

ABOVE. In the winter of 1970, two Alco DL701s with DW&P #3608 leading, await the brakeman to throw the turnout. With -8° weather, he can't be too happy with his job. The black and white sign identifies the junction as being a crossing with Lake Superior Terminal & Transfer Railway. It has 24 miles of track and owns and operates Union Depot at Superior, Wisconsin.

RIGHT. Alco DL701 #3608 and sister #3600 are in their original DW&P colors in this March, 1964 scene. They have just come in from a freight run and await servicing at Duluth.

"Delivered with Pride" is the new DW&P slogan applied to an old caboose at Duluth in 1979. Sandwiched between two newer ones, #79159 still looks good even with the unusual step guards.

Elgin, Joliet & Eastern

Elgin, Joliet & Eastern 2,000 hp Baldwin center cab diesel #924 sits on an interchange track at Griffith, Indiana on October 29, 1966. Locomotive #924 was built in 1948 and had its worn out engines replaced by EMD engines in 1956.

The roundhouse at Joliet, Illinois in 1982 is home to EJ&E #702 GP-38-2, a 2,000 hp locomotive built in 1972 and #607 SD-9, a 1,750 hp engine which was formerly DM&IR #133. The "J" was one of the first Class I railroads to dieselize, retiring its last steam locomotive in October of 1949. Unlike some other railroads, the "J" saved the round-house and modified it for servicing diesels.

In 1950 the EJ&E purchased Baldwin's four unit DR-4-4 Sharknose demonstrator. However, the units proved unsatisfactory and were sold to the B&O in 1955. Seldom photographed, here we see in an oil painting what they might have looked like, speeding eastward through Griffith, Indiana on a cold winter night in 1952. *Painting through courtesy of owner Bill Bedell*

With 2,000 hp Baldwin center cab #921 leading, a train comes upgrade from Joliet, Illinois in October of 1972. Built in 1948, the center cab was re-engined by EMD in 1956.

Between 1937-1940, four Alco Model HH, 660 hp diesels were built for the "J" and designed by Otto Kuehler. Locomotive #211 is shown at the Waukegan, Illinois roundhouse in April of 1962.

Ten Baldwin-built (1941-1944) 1,000 hp Model VO switchers served faithfully on the "J". Here #481 is shown at Joliet in December of 1963 on the service track in the good company of center cab units.

Veteran #270, the first of three 660 hp Model VO switchers built between 1940-1941, sits alongside the roundhouse in Joliet, in October of 1963. The #270 was an unusual diesel, having a front end ventilating opening, much different than other diesel switchers. In 1964 it was converted into a slug or trailer, which consisted of a ballasted locomotive frame mounted over regular trucks powered with traction motors driven from a cab-powered diesel.

Erie-Lackawanna

The crossing gate goes up as a southbound Erie-Lackawanna freight train clears the highway in Griffith, Indiana. No mistaking the caboose design—it's Erie without a doubt. Barely noticeable in front of the first automobile at the gate are the Grand Trunk Western tracks. The tracks in front of the GTW depot at left are EJ&E, and an interchange track is in the foreground. In spite of the lack of snow in December of 1971, the sign over the road proclaims the Christmas season.

Coming off the main line at Griffith in October of 1972, E-L #3310 swings onto the EJ&E interchange track and will head west to pick up freight cars. On lease from Norfolk & Western, #3310 was built by GE in 1969 as a 3,300 hp U33C. A rare storm blowing off Lake Michigan has given Griffith, Indiana the first snowfall of the season.

The main attraction at Dearborn Street Station in Chicago on this day in May, 1961 is Grand Trunk Western #6322 4-8-4 ready to depart with a fantrip special. Ironically, the Erie PAs hardly get a glance from the fans; that will change when the PAs dwindle in number. In between the veterans, a Santa Fe switcher prepares to take cars to the 18th Street coach yard.

The *Lake Cities* Chicago-New York passenger train powered with Alco PAs, rapidly approaches 130th Street on the south side of Chicago on February 25, 1967. These were the last PAs on the railroad.

In 1967, with the best looking power around, the *Lake Cities* with PAs prepares to depart Dearborn Street Station, Chicago. On the extreme left is a Santa Fe switcher assigned to coach yard duties. Next to the PAs is the GTW *Maple Leaf* ready to depart for Toronto. In the foreground, Chicago & Western Indiana Alco RS-1 makes a cloud of smoke as it begins its work in the terminal.

A pair of EMD E-8 diesel passenger units pass Chicago's 21st Street crossing on their way to Dearborn Street Station. There they will couple to the cars of the *Lake Cities* and head out shortly for New York City. A Pennsy switcher hidden behind the E-8s pushes a string of passenger cars to the coach yard in this May, 1968 scene.

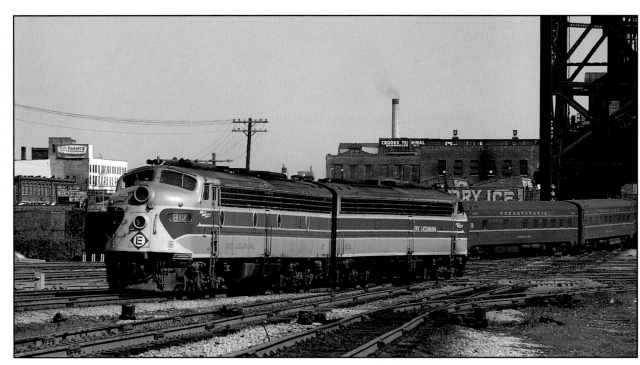

Canting sharply into a curve, Erie-Lackawanna #2512, a 2,500 hp GE model U25B, takes its trailer train southward through Pullman Junction in February of 1968. At that time, Pullman Junction had a number of railroads using its crossings including B&O, C&O, C&WI, E-L, Monon, RI and Norfolk & Western.

This is E-L #2512 northbound through Griffith. A freight with its caboose is ready to depart south from the yard track. F-7A 1,500 EMD diesel #7131 and freight train is ready to move north as soon as #2512 clears in this April, 1974 scene. It's hard to believe this entire railroad is gone now and only a sea of weeds remain.

As the crossing guard looks it over, #3310, a leased N&W GE U33C diesel built in 1969, leads its train past the tower at Griffith on October 18, 1972. It has crossed the C&O, is now crossing the EJ&E, and is about to cross GTW and PC. A light snow, rare this early, offers contrast to the picture.

Green Bay & Western

Kewaunee, Green Bay & Western Alco FA-1s #501 and #502 built in 1947, head for the railroad car ferry dock at Kewaunee, Wisconsin in September of 1949. Both units were retired in 1959. Locomotive #501 was scrapped in February of 1964, and #502 was scrapped in February of the next year.

GB&W #313 eases out of the enginehouse onto the turntable at Green Bay in August of 1976. The #313 was built by Alco as a 2,400 hp DL24 in 1965, using parts salvaged from FAs scrapped at the Green Bay shops.

GB&W diesels hurry a freight eastward near Luxemburg, Wisconsin in October of 1972. The first unit, #309, was built by Alco in 1960, the first RS-27 anywhere. It was scrapped in March of 1986.

In a pleasing color scheme, Alco FA-1 #503 comes off the turntable at Green Bay in April of 1951. Built in 1949, it was retired in 1959, a very short life beset with mechanical and engine problems.

Coming westward from the ferry terminal at Kewaunee, KGB&W diesel #309 and GB&W diesel #310 round a curve on their way to Green Bay in May of 1973.

Locomotive #315, a 3,000 hp C430 diesel, was delivered from Alco in February of 1968. Here it awaits assignment at Green Bay in June of 1972. In 1987, #315 was presented to the National Railroad Museum at Green Bay, Wisconsin.

GB&W business car #600 *Roamer* rests under its protective canopy at Green Bay in July of 1968. The elaborate car was built in 1918 at a cost of $200,000 for Joshu Cosden, a wealthy oil man. The Prince of Wales used the car on his tour of the United States in 1924. The car was bought in 1944 by the GB&W and used until 1972 when it was purchased by a private party in Ottawa, Illinois.

Alco demonstrator #415 sits near the GB&W general office building at Green Bay in August of 1966. The all-purpose 1,500 hp diesel was not purchased by the GB&W but the series was purchased by the Southern Pacific and Rock Island. The landmark office building was destroyed by fire on February 11, 1977.

All shined up and no place to go. KGB&W Alco FA-1 #501 sits in the enginehouse at Green Bay in August of 1959. Due to engine and mechanical trouble, the #501 and her sisters have been retired and will be cannibalized for parts to build new diesels.

Cost and maintenance were evidently the reasons for selling business car #600 and replacing it with car #1776. A stretched version of a caboose, #1776 was built by Kraft Steel Fabric Co. of Green Bay in 1972.

GB&W Alco RS-3 #307, a 1,500 hp diesel built in 1955, is in front of the enginehouse at Green Bay in July of 1974. In January, 1975 the #307 was rebuilt to an RS-20 2,000 hp chop nose unit.

GB&W Alco C424 #312, a 2,400 hp diesel built in 1960 is shown at Green Bay in April, 1982. A striking new paint job, complete with vertical stripes and the name of a past president of the GB&W below the cab, commands the attention of all.

The *Trempeleau River Valley Limited* stops at Wisconsin Rapids, Wisconsin in June, 1976. The passenger special consisted of RS-2s #301 and #303, three Algoma Central coaches and the private car *Gritty Palace*.

At Green Bay, former passenger cars still look elegant in the attractive red color of the well-maintained work equipment. When built, the cars had visible truss rods, which kept the bodies from becoming swaybacked. When converted to work cars, heavy metal underframes were installed.

GB&W #315, a 3,000 hp C430 diesel, takes its train across a county road, eastbound to the ferry at Kewaunee in April of 1972.

On a cold and dreary morning in January of 1973, GB&W #309 and #310 with idler flat cars, move toward the hold of Ann Arbor car ferry *Viking*. The modernized *Viking* with its streamlined single funnel is in sharp contrast to the *City of Milwaukee* on the right, which was the last of the classic two stackers.

Gulf, Mobile & Ohio

ABOVE. Doing close to 90 miles per hour, in March, 1970 GM&Os *Limited* streaks south past the depot at Odell, Illinois. The double track main was recently reduced to single track, and the picturesque depot will soon be torn down.

RIGHT. The northbound *Abraham Lincoln* is enveloped in a trail of smoke—and snow kicked up by its speed. Passing through the small town of Lemont, just 25 miles from Chicago, the streamliner is on time on its way to the Windy City in January of 1971.

GM&O #101 and #102A E-7 power the *Limited* in May of 1971 away from the lift bridge spanning the Chicago River in 1971. Foreground tracks lead to the diamonds at 21st Street crossing, Chicago.

At 5:05 p.m. in August of 1968, GM&O #882B F-3 and #102A E-7 units lead the *Abraham Lincoln* out of Chicago's Union Station through a maze of tracks and signals. A New York Central baggage car mars the otherwise perfect color scheme of the train.

Completing its journey on a January day in 1971 from St. Louis, the *Abraham Lincoln* approaches Chicago Union Station. The building on the left on stilts is the tower for controlling all train movements in and out of the station.

GM&O's *Abraham Lincoln* from St. Louis discharges passengers at Joliet in December of 1966. It is the last stop for the streamliner before Chicago, 37 miles away.

In May of 1971, #102 is ready to back up to Union Station in Chicago and pick up cars for the GM&O *Limited*. The two-story brown building to the left of #102 belongs to the Santa Fe and controls the 21st Street crossings of the various railroads.

Southbound *Limited* slows to stop in front of the depot at Pontiac, Illinois. The baggage wagon on the platform is ready to be moved into position, and within minutes the train will resume its journey to St. Louis in this November, 1970 photograph.

A frozen turnout gives the crew of GM&O #1126, an RS-1, and its tank cars, an anxious few moments at Lemont, Illinois. Eventually the lever breaks free of ice, and #1126 clears the main line, which sees numerous freight and passenger trains.

A rare sight on the Chicago & NorthWestern is Amtrak's GM&O *Prairie State* heading north near Milwaukee in January of 1972. A derailment on the Milwaukee main line caused the detour. To the right and out of the picture is Mitchell International Airport, and to the extreme left is the abandoned right-of-way of the Milwaukee Electric interurban line to Racine and Kenosha.

GM&O through freight with SD-40 #908 leading blankets the local switcher and unhappy crew members on the depot platform with a shower of snow spray as it comes south at Lemont, Illinois in February of 1971.

Great Northern

Great Northern's *Western Star* stops briefly at Fargo, North Dakota on a warm afternoon in July, 1959. The beautifully-colored train originated in Chicago, and will terminate its journey in Seattle.

The last operating steam locomotive in the Superior, Wisconsin area was #841 0-8-0, a switcher. Built by Baldwin in March of 1919, #841 was one of 40 Class C-1 heavy duty switchers. All started out as coal burners, but were eventually converted to burn oil. Some punster has chalked up the front of the steamer awaiting assignment in October of 1955. Three years later, it took its place on the scrap tracks with many other Great Northern locomotives, and when the price of scrap iron rose, it was scrapped in 1962.

Brand new EMD 1,500 hp SD-7 #559 has just been delivered to the Great Northern engine track at Minneapolis in June of 1952. Little does the steamer realize that it is to be replaced by that shiny product of EMD.

A pair of EMD SD-7s #6010 and #6007 in the 1970s pull away from their train at the GN-BN ore dock at Superior, Wisconsin. While they are en route to pick up more ore loads, their ore will be dumped into the hold of a freighter for transport to a steel mill in Indiana.

As her crew leans out to await a green signal, Great Northern #402A FT presents a pleasing appearance. Soon it will power its train westward from Minneapolis on this bright day in June of 1952.

GN F unit #316A and adjunct cab unit attempt to keep warm on the enginehouse track. A howling wind from nearby Lake Superior has dropped the temperature below zero on this day in February, 1970 at Superior.

In August, 1959 the conductor of a main line eastbound freight to Fargo, North Dakota waves a greeting to the section foreman at Nolan, North Dakota. The freight is crossing the Devils Lake-Casselton line, which is just behind the tower. Engrossed in the activity, the author's two children are unaware of sitting on the rough stones of the new ballast on the track going to Casselton. Today a sign marks where the tower once stood.

Battling the Grade is an oil painting depicting a daily scene of a long GN freight, slowly moving upgrade in the Cascade Mountains. Nearly-new EMD FT #402D leads the way, wisps of black exhaust the only visible signs of movement.

GN F unit #317C rests between assignments at the Superior roundhouse in February, 1970. This unit was frequently used in passenger service as indicated by the silver buffer and numberboard.

Wearing the new BN-GN merger number, #9728 rounds the curve at the south end of the depot in St. Paul, Minnesota in March 1971. These three old units will soon be replaced by more powerful, new locomotives.

EMD E-7 #510 passenger unit comes onto the turntable at Superior. Soon it will proceed to the cars of the *Gopher* at Duluth, Minnesota and eventually head that train to the Twin Cities.

Sporting both a new merger number and a bright experimental color scheme of white, blue and black in July of 1970, GN-BN F diesel unit #616 with a helper NP B unit behind, moves a freight train west near Detroit Lakes, Minnesota.

A GN-BN lashup consisting of GP-30 #2216, GP-9 #1823 with A and B F units, moves a freight westward out of the former Northern Pacific yard at Minneapolis in March of 1971.

Coming from Devils Lake, North Dakota, a way freight with GP-7 #1555 prepares to stop at Nolan on a July day in 1970. The brakeman is ready to step down and throw a turnout to head the freight east on the main line to Fargo.

Grand Trunk Western

Grand Trunk Western train bound for Muskegon, Michigan in August of 1958 with Pacific #5629 begins to pound over the diamond at Durand. Sheltered from the blast of cinders from the stack by the depot's canopy, some onlookers are brave enough to watch the train's departure.

Durand was a busy place in August of 1958. On the left is a silhouette of a locomotive bound for Detroit. The switcher is on the Port Huron track. Pacific #5629 is on the eastbound Muskegon track. As soon as the switcher is clear, the track barrier in front of #5629 will be swung out of the way, and #5629 will be on its way.

The late afternoon sun gleams on GTW 4-8-4 #6323, waiting for a signal to back up, after delivering a fantrip special to Dearborn Station in Chicago. On a nearby track, a Santa Fe switcher begins to pull cars out to the nearby coach yard. On the far track, assorted cars of the Chicago & Eastern Illinois sit ready for an evening departure. Date: September 2, 1961.

GTW 2-8-2 #4070 crosses the Penn-Central tracks at 21st Street crossing at 9 a.m. on November 3, 1968. The 21-car fantrip special is taking the S curve in stride. At left, a Santa Fe switcher works cars in the coach yard, and on the right, refrigerator cars of various packing companies await assignment.

The first of the popular 4-8-4s used on GTW fantrips, #6322, backs to its train at Dearborn Station in Chicago in May of 1961.

GTW 4-8-2 #6040 gathers speed as it pulls away from the depot at Ionia, Michigan. The open mail car door is catching some breeze on this hot day in August of 1958.

GTW 4-6-2 #5629 is just about to cross Ann Arbor trackage at Durand on its eastward trip to Detroit from Muskegon.

An hour later, #5633 has moved to the depot at Muskegon. Coupled onto its train, the Pacific is ready to depart for Detroit.

Locomotive #5633, a 4-6-2, has just moved away from the coaling tower at Muskegon in this November 1958 photo. It's a miserable day—the rain is stopping, but fog is coming in from nearby Lake Michigan.

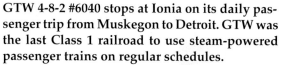

GTW 4-8-2 #6040 stops at Ionia on its daily passenger trip from Muskegon to Detroit. GTW was the last Class 1 railroad to use steam-powered passenger trains on regular schedules.

GTW 4-6-2 #5038 pokes its front end out of the ancient roundhouse at Pontiac, Michigan in August of 1958.

GTW diesel box cab switcher #73 loads cars into the hold of GTW car ferry *Grand Rapids* at Jones Island, Milwaukee in December of 1955. Originally built for the Long Island in 1936 as a gas electric, it was sold to GTW and equipped with Cummins diesels.

With Geep #4901 at the headend, a Chicago-bound GTW passenger train pounds over the C&O-EL and PC diamonds at Griffith, Indiana in June of 1970. The GTW depot at the right has been saved and moved a few blocks away.

Two GTW Geeps work a Detroit-bound passenger train during May of 1971 from Dearborn Station. Soon they will clatter over the PC crossing at 21st Street. Tracks in the foreground belong to Santa Fe and Illinois Central.

GTW 4-6-2 #5629 is ready to depart Durand for Detroit in 195. Locomotive #5629 ran a number of fantrips in the 60s, even furnishing power for the circus train from Baraboo to Milwaukee. Due to some unfortunate events, the handsome Pacific was scrapped in July of 1987.

Sporting the pleasing colors of parent Canadian National, GTW's GP-9 #4907 and F-3 #9010 are serviced at the engine facilities in Chicago in August of 1957.

A maze of trackwork is visible from the tower window at Durand. The GTW and Central Vermont Geeps are just crossing the C&O-EL diamond and are headed west in this May, 1968 picture. The diamond in the foreground belongs to the EJ&E. The crossing guard is standing on Broad Street, and a section of the GTW depot appears at the left.

One of Grand Trunk Western's U4b Class 4-8-4s, built by Lima in 1938, is running late due to a Lake Michigan storm. Locomotive #6409 is rushing the *Maple Leaf* eastward near Durand in this oil painting circa 1950s. Her sister engine, #6405, was one of the last streamlined steamers to operate in the U.S. in the fall of 1959.

Nothing is scrapped on the Greater Winnipeg Water District Railway, which operates between St. Boniface and Indian Bay, Manitoba, a distance of 97.2 miles. The vintage automobile had many miles on the odometer before being converted to a track inspection car. The streamlined power car had a humble beginning as a Mack rail car. Location: St. Boniface, Manitoba, Canada in August of 1959.

Greater Winnipeg Water District Railway

GWW's passenger-baggage gas car #32 sits at the St. Boniface depot in 1959. The car made a daily run between St. Boniface and Indian Bay. In winter months, a snowplow pilot was added to the front end to enable the car to cope with the severe Manitoba weather.

Illinois Central

The sun casts dark shadows on the underside of the hopper car and tender as Illinois Central 2-8-2 #1563 nears Irwin, Illinois. It's on its way to Kankakee on a crisp, cold day in November, 1957.

In this oil painting, the *Argyle & Wooford Flyer*, a fast IC train between Freeport, Illinois and Dodgeville, Wisconsin arrives at Argyle, Wisconsin in October of 1907. Locomotive #1181, a 4-4-0, was built by the Pittsburgh Locomotive Co. in 1880. The depot, built in 1888, was destroyed by fire in 1915.

IC's Chicago to Sioux City *Land O' Corn* led by E-6 #4004 diesel comes off the Fox River bridge near South Elgin, Illinois in March of 1967. A sign of the times, the train has been downgraded to include trailer flats.

Three IC Geeps with #9502 leading round the curve off the Galena River bridge into Galena in May of 1970. Galena was the home of President Ulysses S. Grant.

Leading a trio of IC Geeps, #9378 clips along at a good rate of speed eastbound near Waterloo, Iowa in July of 1963. The level Iowa farmland puts up no obstacle to the train's swift passage.

The lone survivor of pre-electrification of the IC's Chicago commuter line, tank engine #201 is on display at the IC engine terminal in Chicago in September of 1961. The locomotive later would be displayed at Vonachen's Junction near Peoria. There it was part of a railroad-oriented restaurant consisting of two old passenger cars.

With towering Chicago skyscrapers as a backdrop, IC streamliner *City of Miami*, with #2040 at the headend, is ready to depart Central Station. Pity the track section gang working on this windy, cold morning in January of 1972. They have one consolation: their warm truck is just across the tracks.

IC Geep #9147, leading, with a yard switcher trailing, brings a trailer train out of downtown Chicago. It has just crossed the Penn Central's 21st Street diamond and will turn southward. The spectators at right are awaiting a 1971 steam-powered fantrip due to leave shortly from Dearborn Station.

December fog shrouds a southbound Illinois Central Gulf freight on former GM&O track at Chenoa, Illinois. GP-10 #8061 is just crossing TP&W tracks, and in the left background is the abandoned GM&O-TP&W depot.

With a burst of bluish-white exhaust, yard switcher #9204 pulls a string of cars from the IC coach yard in Chicago. A morning fog obscures the many downtown buildings and fresh snow lightens up an otherwise dismal December, 1971 scene.

An IC way freight powered with Geep #9029 passes the Chatsworth, Illinois depot en route to Kankakee from Bloomington in June of 1971. It is about to cross the TP&W main line track.

ABOVE. On a hot August day in 1969, Central Station, Chicago, will soon see a series of movements as a switchman checks for clearance. In minutes, EMD switcher #101 will pick up the business car at right to be put on the rear of the *Seminole* at left.

RIGHT. A trio of IC Geeps led by #8019 rolls past the interlocking tower at Mendota, Illinois in the summer of 1973. The CB&Q track #8019 is crossing, as well as its own track, plus the tower, could use some much-needed maintenance.

Crossing the TP&W track, the *Governor's Special* from Springfield, headed by #4034, swings into the curve approaching the depot at Gilman, Illinois. Here the train will blend into the Chicago main line.

Lake Superior & Ishpeming

The last load of iron ore is dumped into a hopper car at Ishpeming in August of 1960. A little later, veteran 2-8-0 steamer #19 will take its train to the Lake Superior & Ishpeming yard at Marquette.

GE-built U25C #2500, along with sister and Alco RS2 switcher, sit on the engine ready track at Marquette in May of 1973. On later models of the U25C, the big front window was replaced by two smaller windows, due to the high cost of replacement.

As though posed for an official photograph, a vintage box car basks in the early afternoon sun in July of 1960. Two LS&I workers walk from the Marquette roundhouse toward an assignment.

LS&I 2-8-0 #23 sits alone in the once crowded Marquette roundhouse in October of 1962. Its days numbered, #23 still is a picture of power. A distinctive feature of LS&I steamers was the high placement of the headlight on the smokebox front. This enabled the engineer to see over the tops of the ore cars when switching, or to see the caboose lights when in road service.

Alco RSD-12 #1803 in a pleasing color scheme hurries its train along the shoreline of Lake Superior in a scene dated 1965. It has come from Marquette, in right background, and is destined for Lawson, Michigan, 28 miles away.

LS&I 2-8-0 #34, still looking good despite a little weathering in 1960, moves backward at a brisk pace. Crew members on the tender are ready for switching duties in the yard at Marquette. It appears as though iron ore is used to good advantage as yard ballast. This engine is now #734, operated by the Western Maryland Scenic Railroad.

ABOVE. LS&I Alco RS-2 #1611 does some switching in March, 1972 at the railroad's end of the line at Munising. While the engineer cautiously moves the cars into a siding, the brakeman watches as the cars move over the switch.

RIGHT. LS&I maintenance-of-way equipment sits on a siding at Marquette in 1970. The tank car contraption is a weed sprayer, and the converted tender is a steam car, which enables the tank car to spray a killing mixture at a high temperature.

BOTTOM RIGHT. LS&I U25C #2500 helps push a loaded ore train up the ore dock in August of 1973 at Marquette. Once cars are in place, ore is transferred into the hold of the ship below, and #2500 will uncouple and return to the yards.

BELOW. Freshly-painted and lettered bobber caboose has just been moved from the paint shop of the LS&I at Marquette. Date: July 8, 1960.

Manufacturers Railway of St. Louis

The Manufacturers Railway performs bridge service between St. Louis and East St. Louis, Illinois. It also performs switching and terminal service in St. Louis. At the enginehouse in St. Louis, two old but well maintained switchers rest outside. Locomotive #205 Alco S-2 (1,000 hp) was built in 1941 and #210 Alco S-2 (1,000 hp) was built in 1948.

The Manufacturers Railway enginehouse is spacious and clean. The majority of heavy truck repairs are done there using this transfer table shown at the right.

Minneapolis, Northfield & Southern

Minneapolis, Northfield & Southern freight heads from Minneapolis toward Northfield, 45 miles away. Power this day in 1971 is furnished by EMD SW-1200 #32 and #33 switchers built in 1964.

MN&S Baldwin center cab 2,000 hp diesel #23 idles in front of the enginehouse at Minneapolis in March of 1971. Of the five center cabs on the railroad, only #21 and #23 were still in service as of this date.

TOP. This is a close-up view of MN&S center cab diesel #23 in front of the enginehouse at Minneapolis. Crews complained about the noise, the heat and the lack of visibility from the cab. Keeping track alignment was also a problem with these big brutes.

BOTTOM. On the south end of Minneapolis, an afternoon sun highlights the front of EMD SW-1200 MN&S #32. It has just crossed a GN diamond protected by a crash board. Sister #33 helps the freight bound for Northfield as the fireman on #32 enjoys the balmy air of a day in September of 1977.

Monon

TOP. Monon trailer train slowly starts to head into the curve southbound at Pullman Junction, Illinois. All trains are required to stop at the junction. A U23B, #608, and C420 #516 are not necessarily spic and span for the railfan photographers at the right. A workman inspects the track with care as many trains pass through the junction. In this section alone, the Monon shared track with C&WI, N&W and NKP.

MIDDLE. The attractive gold paint still shows through the grime as F-3s #204, #203 and BL-2 #32 sit on the sand track at Lafayette, Indiana engine terminal in March of 1970. When the #203 was damaged in a wreck, it came out of the shops with F-7 style side grills.

BOTTOM LEFT. While photographing NKP steam at Calumet, Illinois in July of 1957, I noticed a strange looking locomotive approaching on nearby Monon tracks. It was my first look at an EMD BL-2 branch line diesel switcher. The Monon had purchased nine of the units in 1948, and at the end of their useful lives, one was saved (#32), which was given to the Kentucky Railroad Museum. Of 59 BL-2s built, #30 was the first of the nine purchased by Monon.

BOTTOM RIGHT. Monon BL-2 #35 waits at Pullman Junction, Illinois in this 1969 scene while the head brakeman walks back to check the tie-on blocks on a trailer flat.

Nickel Plate Road

ABOVE. NKP Berkshire #765, built by Lima in 1944, speeds eastward near Hobart, Indiana. Sending up a gigantic column of white smoke, #765 makes an impressive sight on this below zero day in February of 1958. Locomotive #765 was saved by a Fort Wayne volunteer restoration group.

LEFT. Near Hobart, a reefer train speeds westward in February of 1958 behind a begrimed NKP Berkshire #751. It's a very cold five below zero, as #751 puts on quite a show of power.

Veteran NKP Berkshire #739 is on the turntable at Calumet, Illinois in August, 1957. The last of 24 Class S-1s, #739 was built in 1943 and was equipped for passenger service.

A trio of Berkshires is shown at the coaling tower at Calumet. Calumet was an important location the NKP used to maintain its record-breaking freight train schedules to the East. During John Davin's NKP presidency, a new engine terminal was installed here, costing several million dollars. It had five stalls for steam and three for diesels.

NKP Berkshire #751 is enveloped in steam vapors while awaiting a load of black fuel from the coaling tower at Calumet.

A northbound hot shot freight storms by the east yard engine tracks at Calumet in December of 1957. With the temperature hovering around eight below zero, the fireman dares to peer out from his heated cab at the frigid winter scene passing by.

With full loads of coal, NKP Berkshires #769 and #767 doublehead a freight eastward from Calumet. With the temperature hovering in the mid-90s, the crew of #767 tries to find a cool breeze. The heat in the cab must be almost intolerable.

TOP. A cool December, 1957 wind is blowing in from Lake Michigan, and NKP Berkshire #752, its headlights aglow, is ready to leave the Calumet coaling tower. The engineer has already made an inspection of #752's running gear with his lantern, per the snake-like patterns of light.

BOTTOM. During a series of fantrips on the Toledo, Peoria & Western, NKP Berkshire #765 was used in pusher service. It makes a dramatic sight as it helps a freight upgrade at Washington, Illinois bound for Effner in May of 1980.

New York Central

St. Louis, "Gateway to the West," is a very busy railroad city in October of 1966. A pair of NYC EMD E-8s (#4055 and #4053) lead a trailer train around a sharp curve. In the background, a Terminal Railroad Association Alco-GE S-2 switcher, #571, works with a N&W Geep. In back of #571, a portion of an REA express car appears. This car was once a World War II U.S. Army bunk car built by Pullman.

NYC 2,000 hp EMD E-7A #4014 leads a foursome of power units with an eastbound freight through South Bend. A lone switcher works at the right, close to the abandoned passenger station. At left looms the empty shell of the once busy Studebaker automobile plant. Date: June, 1970.

NYC #1491 Class H5 2-8-2 rests at Earl Park, Indiana on a cold day in December of 1953. Looking a trifle weary, #1491 still gives a good impression of heavy power, capable of moving tonnage at a good rate of speed on this heavy traffic main line between Chicago and Cincinnati.

Just 10 years old, NYC Niagara Class Slb #6003 meets an untimely end at a scrap yard in Gary, Indiana in July, 1957. Locomotive #6003 was one of 27 super power, modern steam locomotives built by Alco in 1945-46 for the NYC. With EMD E-8s rapidly taking over passenger service on the eastern end of the railroad, the Niagaras were gradually bumped to commuter and freight service and then quietly scrapped. Ironically on an adjoining track, another super power modern locomotive awaits the torch. Locomotive #1611 Class H8 2-6-6-6 Allegheny (built by Lima in 1941), also had a short life.

NYC passenger train #341 from Indianapolis to St. Louis comes to a stop at Mattoon, Illinois in November of 1963. Locomotive #5933 GP-9 with 1,750 hp built in 1955 is the power for this daily train. Steady, drizzling rain keeps passengers waiting to board in the shelter of the station canopy.

At Mattoon, both NYC conductor and car attendant watch a late passenger arrive in the green station wagon. That was no problem, as many passengers are still boarding.

ABOVE. The Bay City wayfreight comes into Mackinaw City, Michigan in 1965 with an EMD GP-9 at the headend. The cars are destined for St. Ignace via the railroad car ferry *Chief Wawatam.* The depot at the right is a reminder of days before the Straits' bridge was built, when hundreds of passengers detrained to ride ferries to Mackinac Island and St. Ignace.

LEFT. In this circa 1951 oil painting, NYC's *Lake Shore Limited* rounds the curve coming into Englewood Station on the south side of Chicago. The December night air is crisp, and the steam and smoke from the Hudson will soon spread along the platform, obscuring everything in sight. After a brief stop to pick up passengers, the train will be on its way east. The Class J-3a Hudson finds no difficulty in hauling the heavyweight coaches and sleepers along the Water Level Route to Boston and New York City.

A NYC towerman waves a friendly greeting from the warmth of his doorway as the Indianapolis-bound *James Whitcomb Riley* roars by Swanington, Indiana on a cold day in December, 1953. At one time the Chicago, Attica & Southern interchanged and crossed here, but now only the NYC uses the crossing and interchange to service nearby towns.

Norfolk & Western

ABOVE. Filling the length of the turntable, N&W Class A #1204 is ready to be turned at the engine facilities at Columbus, Ohio in November of 1957. The huge 2-6-6-4 articulated was built by the N&W Roanoke Shops in 1937. Sister #1206 was viewed by thousands at the New York World's Fair in 1940.

RIGHT. N&W #8485, a GE U30B, and #3464, an EMD GP-7, (former Wabash #464), lead a freight around a curve at Pullman Junction. It's hard to believe automobiles like these were transported without vandalism protection in January of 1972.

Clattering over the GM&O crossing at Springfield, Illinois in 1973, N&W #506 GP-9 leads a ballast train westward. Its destination is the Mississippi River where severe flooding has required sand bagging and ballast to keep the tracks from washing away. The tower operator can count on being busy with such trains during the next few days.

N&W #2231 (ex-NKP #231) EMD SW-7 switcher brings a transfer freight through a series of crossings at Pullman Junction. The crossings are protected by flagged gates by day and red lights by night. All trains are required to stop before proceeding through the junction.

Northern Pacific

In August of 1962 at Detroit Lakes, Minnesota, Northern Pacific #6005A leads the way as it pounds the Soo Line crossing on its way to the Twin Cities. Locomotive #6005A, a 1,500 hp EMD F-3A, was built in 1948.

NP #1839, a Class W5 2-8-2, gets ready to move off a turntable under the eyes of a group of railfans at Minneapolis in August of 1956. The engine was one of 25 W5s built by Alco in 1923. This class was the biggest and best of the NP 2-8-2s. In 1925, a sister engine, #1844, hauled a freight from the Pacific Coast to the Twin Cities without uncoupling from the train.

A trio of NP F-3s, in an attractive color scheme, is on display at Fargo, North Dakota on a very warm day in June, 1962. The lead unit, #6001A, is sporting a "Radio Equipped" sign depicting the NP's determination to be right in tune with the latest safety innovations.

On a winter morning, NP #2675, Class A4, a 4-8-4 built in 1941, crosses the Soo Line at Detroit Lakes, Minnesota on its way to the Twin Cities. A Soo Line freight from Winnipeg is waiting for the towerman to change the distant semaphore signal (hidden behind #2675) from *stop* to *proceed*. This oil painting was based on several photos taken during visits to the towerman.

NP Budd railcar B-32 arrives at Fargo on its daily run from Winnipeg in August of 1962. The B-32 was originally built for the Western Pacific in 1950 as #376. WP sold it to NP in April of 1962.

One of the last assignments for NP #1545, a Class W 2-8-2, was to haul a fantrip around the Minneapolis area in August of 1956. While fans toured the engine and shop facilities at Minneapolis, #1545 sat under a bridge, blissfully ignoring the sign attached to the bridge support. Built in the early 1900s, the Ws were the heaviest motive power of that period.

With just a 10 minute schedule stop, baggage is hurriedly put in the baggage car of the westbound *Mainliner* at Fargo in July of 1970. The BN-NP merger has brought ex-NP #6511C F-7, now BN #9782, to lead the train, destined for Tacoma, Washington.

Power rests between assignments at the Staples, Minnesota engine yard in July of 1970. On the left, Alco RS-11 #916 is grimy compared to EMD GP-9 #324, which appears to have had a recent paint job. Another GP-9, #1952, is coupled to #324. The bell and hanger on #916 appears to have come off a steam locomotive, while the bell on #324 appears to be quite new and kept polished.

At Superior, Wisconsin, NP #1795, a 2-8-2 Class W3, releases a column of steam as it drifts toward a switchman. Once routed through the switch to the main line, #1795 will head its long freight to Ashland, Wisconsin.

At Minneapolis, the engineer inspects the air pump on NP #1574, a Class W 2-8-2 built in the early 1900s. Stephenson valve gear makes good use of the slanted cylinder castings, a trademark of the Ws. To extend the engine's range, the tender height was raised to carry more coal.

The crew of #2457, a Class T-1 2-6-2, enjoys a lunch break from switching chores at Minneapolis in 1957. A versatile engine, 150 were built during 1906 and 1907 and used in switching, local and main line service. Many parts of the 2-6-2s were interchangeable with the early 2-8-2s, thus serving to prolong the life of both classes.

ABOVE. Alco RS-11 #904 heads BN-NP freight from Superior to Ashland, Wisconsin. Overhead a GN road diesel backs away from a load of iron ore it has just delivered to the dock. BELOW. NP's *Mainliner* comes west past the handsome depot at Casselton, North Dakota. Luckily, Minnesota's numerous clouds parted long enough to photograph this August, 1962 scene.

Equipped with a steel underframe, a classic wood caboose readily bears the pressure of #1647, a Class W 2-8-2, as it pushes a freight upgrade in 1957 from Duluth to Minneapolis. The boiler of veteran #1647 still gleams from a recent overhaul, which was unusual, as the end of steam operations on the NP was near.

Post merger BN-NP power moves on the east curve out of St. Paul, headed for servicing in March of 1971. BN lead unit #9802 F-9 was NP #6700C and trailing unit in BN colors #9782 F-7 was NP 6511C.

With the temperature below zero, a hostler hurries to the warm cab of NP F-7 #6015A. Earlier he had moved sister F-7 #6015D away from servicing at the sand tower. Sheltered by the roundhouse from a stiff wind blowing off the lake at Duluth, an Alco-GE Class S-4 1,000 hp switcher gets ready to move out to work the nearby yard in February of 1970.

Two F-7As, one F-7B and a Geep power a 1962 westbound freight at Detroit Lakes. Lead unit #6012A has just crossed the Winnipeg-Minneapolis Soo Line track. Today the tower is gone with control of the crossing handled from Minneapolis.

EMD F-7 BN #740, former NP #6016A and two NP B units are joined by a GN A unit, awaiting more cars. On a nearby track, EMD Class SW-1200 switcher is ready to assume its duties, once #740 departs the yard at Minneapolis.

Northwestern Steel & Wire

ABOVE. Former GTW #8380, a 0-8-0 switcher built by Baldwin in 1919, works the Northwestern Steel & Wire mill at Sterling, Illinois in October of 1967. Upon arrival at the mill in the early 60s, the first two digits of the engine numbers were removed, thus #8380 became #80. The switchers were used until early December 1980. Locomotive #80 went to the Illinois Railway Museum.

RIGHT. Ex-GTW #8373, a 0-8-0 switcher built by Baldwin in 1929, works the west end of the Northwestern Steel & Wire mill at Sterling on a fall day. Shown as a coal burner, #73 was later converted to oil. In 1981, #73 was donated to the P.W. Dillon Museum in Sterling. One GTW switcher, #27, was sold to Bandana Square in St. Paul, Minnesota in 1983, and another, #76, was sold to the Amboy, Illinois Depot Museum in 1981.

Pennsylvania

Baldwin-built RF-16 #9728 freight diesel, built in 1952, idles at the Pennsylvania engine facilities in Pittsburgh in July of 1961. Because of its unique design, it was nicknamed "Sharknose," as was the passenger version.

Big, husky GG-1 #4905 electric, designed by the famous industrial stylist Raymond Loewy, accelerates a passenger train toward New York from the Wilmington, Delaware station in June of 1967.

ABOVE. The *Pennsylvania Limited* from New York waits for a signal before proceeding into Chicago Union Station on a December day in 1971. With the Penn-Central merger and Amtrak takeover of passenger service, the *Limited* and cars in the adjacent coach yard show a mixture of equipment from various railroads.

LEFT. At Enola, Pennsylvania near Harrisburg, GE E-44 electric locomotives #4434 and #4429 share yard tracks with a GG-1 passenger unit. The 4,400 hp units were built specifically for freight train service.

Penn Central GE U28C #6529 is the lead unit in a trio of power bringing a long freight into Chicago. Northbound in the morning sun, it is ready to go over the diamonds at the 21st Street crossing in this 1971 scene.

ABOVE. Pennsy GG-1 #4863 built in the Altoona shops of the Pennsy in 1938, awaits a signal to couple onto its train at Trenton, New Jersey in July of 1961. A total of 139 of these fast, reliable locomotives were built between 1934 and 1943.

LEFT. A crew member prepares to step down from the cab of EMD F-7 #9878, a 1,500 hp freight unit built in 1952. Facing #9878 on an adjoining track is Alco FPA-1 #9605, a 1,500 hp unit built in 1948. Switchers from various builders make up the rest of the power at this engine facility at Pittsburgh in 1961.

Penn Central GP-38 #7821 switches freight cars into the hold of railroad car ferry *Chief Wawatam* at Mackinaw City on Michigan's lower Peninsula in February of 1972. Once loaded, *Chief Wawatam*, a coal burner built in 1911, will steam across the Straits of Mackinac to St. Ignace on the upper peninsula. There, the load of 26 cars will be transferred to the Soo Line.

The big lift bridge over the Chicago River dwarfs a transfer freight going over the diamonds at 21st Street crossing in Chicago. The short freight is headed by Pennsy GP-35 #2356 and two CB&Q Geeps.

Emitting black exhaust, Penn Central #8026, an Alco DL721, leads a westbound freight down a well-ballasted right-of-way near Hammond, Indiana. Part way back, automotive carriers sway with the forward speed of the train. The fully-covered auto carrier is still a few years away.

Pennsy E-8A #4298 with a trailing B unit, moves toward Chicago Union Station in May of 1968. Later in the afternoon a switcher will begin the task of moving the passenger cars, in the yard at the right, onto assigned tracks in the station.

Baldwin-built Sharknose passenger units rest at the end of the line at Point Pleasant, New Jersey in July of 1961. While #5782 has the older pin striping and lettering, #5780 has been recently repainted in a more modern single stripe, large letters and numbers. Both have the roof antenna, a Pennsy trademark.

PRR #70, a Chicago to Cincinnati passenger train, comes out of the lift bridge shadows and is just about to go across the diamonds at 21st Street crossing in May, 1971. Single unit E-8A #4299 is more than enough power for this short train.

A pair of Pennsy Alco RS-3 switchers, led by #8594, move a string of freight cars in the classification yard at Pittsburgh in July of 1961. Spoiling an otherwise handsome diesel design, the unsightly roof antennas appear as gigantic handrails.

The *Manhattan Limited* departs Chicago's Union Station in October of 1958. Powered by #5763, an EMD E-8, it is heavy with mail and baggage cars as it snakes its way through the switches at the entrance to the station. Soon it will gather speed for its daily trip to New York City.

The Senator, en route from Washington, D.C. to New York City in 1967, stops at Wilmington to discharge and pick up passengers. Headed by a GG-1, the train has come in on time, a normal procedure for this dependable type of electric power.

While a photographer records the 1960 action, Pennsy FM C-Liner #9453 with its B units slowly growls eastward around Horseshoe Curve near Altoona. With the weather hot and humid, the fireman is glad to be able to catch a breeze through the open side cab window.

ABOVE. While a baggage man moves a package in the car, the Wilmington station baggage handler waits to hand up the remainder of the baggage and packages. Then, Pennsy's *Midday Congressional* will be on its way to New York City. Date: June, 1967.

LEFT. While the towerman waves to the engineer, the fireman waves to the photographer as Pennsy GE U30B, with #2866 leading, heads a freight east at Kouts, Indiana in June of 1975. It is crossing the diamond of the Erie-Lackawanna whose depot appears in the distance.

In electrified territory, invader EMD GP-35 #2281 leads a 1967 eastbound freight around a curve a few miles east of Lancaster, Pennsylvania. A slight haze of engine exhaust begins to drift slowly toward U.S. Highway 30.

Rock Island

ABOVE. The town of Peoria, Illinois wanted Pacific #886 for display, as it was the last engine operating out of the city in March of 1952. However, it had been scrapped, so Rock Island renumbered Pacific #887 to #886. Before being displayed, it is shown with GP-7 #1250 at Peoria, in July of 1963.

LEFT. Rock Island GM LWT-12 Aerotrain #2, a locomotive with two cars, sits at the C&NW yard in Butler, Wisconsin in September of 1966. A little later it will be moved to the National Railroad Museum in Green Bay.

Rock Island EMD E-6A #630, a 2,000 hp passenger diesel built in 1941, brings a suburban train into Joliet. It is just about to cross the GM&O and Santa Fe diamond and come to a stop beyond the diamond at Union Station in April of 1973.

Eastbound freight with GE U28B #240 and GE #215 is just crossing the diamond at Joliet. Just behind #240 is the magnificent Union Station, which served the Rock Island, GM&O and Santa Fe railroads.

GM LWT-12 Aerotrain #3 locomotive is being worked on at LaSalle Street Station in March 1964. One of three Rock Island Aerotrains serving the suburbs between Chicago and Joliet, #3 was donated to the National Museum of Transport in September of 1966.

Early afternoon is a busy time for Chicago's LaSalle Street Station in this October, 1966 scene. EMD AB-6 #751 is outbound with a passenger train for Joliet, while EMD F-7A #675, built in 1949, is inbound from Joliet. With just a one car train, the conductor is waving the engineer to the station. A longer train would have to be backed in by a whistle signal from the rear car. On the left, EMD SW-8 #814, built in 1952, waits for #751 to clear before bringing out the trailer flat cars. Two other switchers behind the passenger trains await their assignments.

Heading west, E-8 #657 leads big power around the sweeping curve at Bureau Junction, Illinois. In the foreground, tracks branch off from the main line to Peoria. Locomotive #657 was originally C&NW E-7 #5007B built by EMD in 1945, then purchased by UP and rebuilt to E-8 #925 in 1952. In 1969 it was purchased by the Rock Island and numbered #657. Strangely, it and the B units remained in UP colors.

As a heavy wet snow clings to the countryside, an Iowa Terminal electric locomotive waits for Rock Island EMD GP-40 3,000 hp #342 freight locomotive with its freight to clear the crossing at Clear Lake, Iowa in March of 1971.

GP-7 #1283 and GP-40 #382 lead an eastbound freight past colorful red and yellow bi-level suburban coaches at Joliet, Illinois in November of 1971. These modern coaches were the last desperate effort for the railroad to boost a money-losing task, which eventually failed.

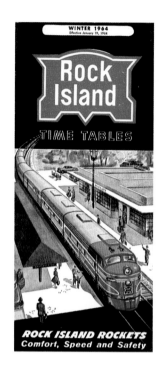

Rock Island passenger train from Rock Island comes past Joliet Union Station on its way to Chicago in May of 1970. The nicely-painted headend power is #650, a 2,250 hp E-8, built in 1952. The train is considerably shorter than in previous years when it made its first run to Denver.

Alco DL-415, a 1,500 hp switcher, idles between assignments in the Rock Island yard at Chicago in May of 1968. One of nine units built for the Rock Island, #424 will soon begin the task of assembling trailer-filled flats for shipment westward.

The engineer of Rock Island GP-7 #1265 looks back at the brakeman checking brakeshoes on a hopper car. The eastbound train has been stopped for a long time, as the tank truck driver has opened his door to escape the heat of the cab.

BELOW. An odd-looking #750, one of two EMD AB-6 units, was built for the *Rocky Mountain Rocket* Colorado Springs connection. Original power of 1,000 hp was eventually upgraded to 2,000 hp. Toward the end, the two units were used in Chicago-Joliet suburban operation. Here, #750 awaits servicing at the Rock Island engine terminal at Chicago in spring of 1972. On the next track is veteran EMD NW-2 switcher #4904, built in 1944, and EMD GP-7 #1277, built in 1952.

A far cry from its former glory, the *Golden State* comes to a stop at Ottawa, Illinois. The westbound train has trailer flats included in its consist, the latest mixed train version of rail progress. The lonely, weed-covered platform is devoid of waiting passengers. Only the train order signal mast indicates the depot is still active in this 1970 scene. Headend power is a veteran 2,000 hp EMD E-7A built in 1946.

Eastbound Rock Island freight is just crossing the diamond at Joliet. Two EMD FP-7s and lone Alco-GE FA-1 #129, power this fast freight from Rock Island. The chimney of the tower, which governs traffic through this busy intersection, is shown above the roof of #129. Two years later in 1965, #129 was traded along with other FA-1s to EMD for new units.

Eastbound Rock Island freight battles a blinding snowstorm at Clear Lake, Iowa in March of 1971. The massive power is GE U33B #288 built in 1969 and showcasing 3,300 hp. This storm eventually stopped highway traffic for two days in the vicinity.

LEFT. A Joliet-bound suburban train leaves Chicago in May of 1968 behind EMD AB-6, unit #751. At the right is Rock Island's coach and freight yard, and around the curve is 16th Street tower and the crossing with PC, IC and C&NW. BELOW. Brand new EMD GP-38-2s, resplendent in a white and blue color scheme, await assignment at the Chicago engine terminal in November of 1976.

With horn blasting, GP-7 #1283 bears down on a country road west of Ottawa, Illinois. The westbound freight is leaving a trail of dust behind as it makes its way to Rock Island in May of 1970.

ABOVE. Rock Island E-8A #643 built in 1949 and originally EMD demonstrator #952, is the power as Train #6-8 from Rock Island comes past the Joliet depot platform. An early wet snow has blanketed the area in a Christmas card setting on this October 28, 1972.

RIGHT. Located about 10 miles south of downtown Chicago is Pullman Junction where the C&WI, B&O, Belt Railway of Chicago, E-L, Monon, N&W(NKP)RI and Wabash cross. All trains are required to stop here before crossing the diamonds. The engineer of RI freight engine #122, and F-7A built in 1951, confers with the junction operator.

Soo Line

Soo Line EMD F-7 #214, in an attractive chocolate brown and cream color scheme, comes uphill from Waukesha, Wisconsin and within seconds will cross the Milwaukee Road main line at Duplainville. It's August of 1961.

At Waukesha, Soo Line 2-8-0 #432 heads north in November, 1949 on a switch run to pick up more cars. At the right is the ancient roundhouse, which in recent years saw a locomotive go through a wall, as evidenced by the newer brick section. Down the track at left is an elevated crossing shanty, which controls the highway gates below.

ABOVE. While the headend crew switches in a Railway Express car, all is quiet at the sleeping car end of #17, the *Laker*. The train has come from Chicago and is scheduled to end its run early the next morning at Duluth. Most of the time the *Laker* had sleepers for Ashland, Wisconsin and Minneapolis, and at times, a sleeper to Duluth. A sleeper-diner was also operated through to Duluth. All equipment was of conventional heavyweight construction.

RIGHT. Departing Minneapolis for St. Paul and Dresser, Wisconsin, Soo Line Train #62 steams majestically along on June 1, 1952, leaving a heavy plume of coal smoke drifting over its cars. Pacific #2708, a Class H-21, is nicely polished, but was hurriedly pressed into service before work on the tender could have been accomplished.

Freshly painted GP-30 #4301 slowly leads a southbound freight through a switch. Soo Line has converted most of the Milwaukee-Twin Cities main line to single track with passing sidings, such as this one at Kilbourn East.

Competition from airplanes and expressways gradually enticed passengers away from Soo Line's *Laker*. The last northbound run of #3, the *Laker*, between Chicago and Superior, Wisconsin stops briefly at Waukesha on January 15, 1965. Inaugurated as the *Laker* in 1951, the train had old style heavyweight equipment, but with modernized interiors.

Soo Line Alco-GE FA-1 #2221 revs up its engines in preparation for moving to its train in the nearby yard. It's a cold, but clear night with a hard crust forming on the fresh snow outside the Shops Yard office at North Fond du Lac in January, 1950. This oil painting is based on several night photos.

A baggage-combine brings up the rear of the last northbound *Laker* at Waukesha on January 15, 1965. The cold night has discouraged fans who had wanted to pay their homage to this last passenger train operating between Chicago and Superior.

SD-60M #6062, wearing the solid red color scheme of the Soo Line, comes out of the new Kilbourn-West siding at milepost 200 in July of 1992, about seven miles north of the Wisconsin Dells. The ex-Milwaukee main line double track had recently been reduced to single track with passing sidings installed like at Kilbourn-West. Locomotive #6062 is headed north toward the Twin Cities.

The twilight sky silhouettes Soo Line tower, train order semaphores and a distant signal at Detroit lakes, Minnesota where the Soo crosses the main line of the NP. There's not much activity now, but in the early morning hours the *Winnipeger* passes in both directions. Not shown are the hundreds of mosquitoes that attacked the photographer during this time exposure in August of 1962.

Making a transfer run, 3,000 hp GE U30-C #807 built in 1968, utilizes Illinois Central tracks in downtown Chicago. On the station platform at the left, passengers are awaiting an IC electric train to take them swiftly to the suburbs in August of 1969.

The engineer gently pushes the last string of freight cars into the hold of Ann Arbor railroad car ferry *Viking* near downtown Manitowoc. GP-7 #408 is well suited for this daily, year-round job. In the left background is the stately courthouse, and on the right, one of the very old Soo Line outside-braced wood box cars. Weather permitting, the *Viking* will make the trip across Lake Michigan to Ludington in five hours.

Soo Line GP-30, a 2,250 hp locomotive built in 1963, negotiates a sharp curve at Slinger, Wisconsin. Shortly it will cross the Milwaukee tracks (Milwaukee-Berlin line) and head south through Waukesha to Chicago.

ABOVE. Storming over the Milwaukee Road diamond at Duplainville, Soo Line GE U30-C #800 heads a northbound freight toward Fond du Lac. The fast moving train kicks up powdery snow, much to the dismay of the photographer, who had to wait for the entire train to pass before seeking the warmth of the tower. Date: February, 1984.

LEFT. Former Duluth, South Shore & Atlantic Alco RS-1, a veteran road switcher which has retained its original number under Soo Line management, works in the industrial section of Manitowac in October of 1966.

Wasting no time, SD-40 #749, a 3,000 hp unit built in 1969, leads its train northbound down Byron Hill. Within half an hour, it will be in the Soo Line yard at North Fond du Lac where some of the cars will be switched out for local distribution The rest will continue to the Twin Cities.

Daily Train #2 from the Twin Cities to Chicago crosses a county road south of Waukesha. Pacific #730 Class H-3 does an effortless job with this four-car train in July of 1952.

Northbound Soo Line freight gets the green light from the tower operator at Burlington, Wisconsin and soon it will clatter over the Milwaukee Road (Sturtevant, Wisconsin-Kansas City line) diamond, pass through Burlington and head for Waukesha and the Twin Cities.

Afternoon shadows fall on the closed depot and power units of a Soo Line freight westbound at Granville, Wisconsin in November of 1964. Head-end power is EMD GP-9, built in 1955. Coming from Milwaukee it will connect with the main line at Rugby Junction, Wisconsin.

The brakeman climbs yard switcher #2106 as his engineer converses with the fireman of road engine #2408. The long freight, powered by EMD GP-9 #2408, has just come into Shops Yard at North Fond du Lac. Yard switcher Alco-GE S-2 #2106 waits to remove and add cars in #2408s consist in August of 1965.

EMD NW-1A #2100, a 900 hp switcher built in 1938, was the oldest Soo Line diesel still working in July of 1965. At Burlington, Wisconsin #2100 sits without crew during a lunch break. Soon #2100 will be put to work, setting out and picking up cars on the various industrial sidings.

Yard switcher #371 smokes up the sky, as it and companion #2124 make up a train of cars in Shops Yard at North Fond du Lac in February, 1966. Locomotive #371 is an Alco-GE product, Class RS-2, 1,500 hp diesel built in 1949. Its helper, #2124, is an EMD product, Class SW-1200 diesel built in 1955.

Traveling over Milwaukee Road rails from North Milwaukee, Soo Line F-7 #2229B with a companion, brings its train past Grand Avenue tower, in Milwaukee. The tower controls tracks to North Milwaukee and the main line to the west (out of picture to the left). Just behind #2229B, a Milwaukee Road switcher has just set out a car and is ready to come back on the main track.

With a blast of heavy black smoke, Soo Line Train #2 from the Twin Cities to Chicago, leaves Slinger, Wisconsin in July, 1951. The last coach of the train is crossing the Milwaukee Road line (Milwaukee-Berlin). The ornamental depot at left was shared by both railroads.

Bearing down fast on a rural crossing near Sussex, Wisconsin in February of 1972, Soo Line EMD GP-30 #707 emits a cloud of black exhaust. Unfortunately, the unique swinging crossing signal and sign are about gone from the railroad scene. Date: February 1972.

Just south of Fond du Lac, Soo Line EMD F-3, 1,500 a hp unit and its helpers, begin the long ascent of Byron Hill. Locomotive #2200-A had the distinction of being the first F unit on the Soo Line in 1948. This photograph was taken 17 years later.

The last operating steam crane on the Soo goes about its job of cleaning up the right of way near Sussex in March of 1969.

Terminal Railroad Association

A Terminal Railroad Association switcher, #1232, awaits work at the engine terminal in St. Louis. The TRRA handles about 70 percent of all St. Louis rail traffic, as well as connecting with barge lines operating on the Mississippi River.

Alco-GE S-2 units #569 and #570, built in 1949, furnish power for a trailer train of new automobiles moving north in October 1966. This elevated section of the TRRA is on the west bank of the Mississippi River at St. Louis, and connects with two railroad bridges to East St. Louis. With large capacity yards and nearly 341 miles of track, the TRRA is more than adequately equipped to handle traffic quickly through the St. Louis gateway.

Toledo, Peoria & Western

Toledo, Peoria & Western #900 helps bring a 1980 freight eastward on a rainy day at Crescent City, Illinois. The #900 is an EMD GP-35 equipped with Alco trucks from an RS-2 trade-in. In 1950 the TP&W was merged with the Pennsy and Santa Fe but allowed to operate as an independent railroad. Thus Pennsy and Santa Fe locomotives were sometimes used to fill power shortages.

On a bleak winter day in February of 1972, TP&W #402, an Alco RS-11 and #206, an Alco RS-2, and caboose are at Effner, Indiana, the eastern end of the TP&W line. Here, Pennsy crews will man the engines and run them into the Pennsy yard approximately 60 miles east at Logansport to pick up cars.

Alco RS-2 #204 has just put together a train at the big yard in East Peoria. Locomotive #204, built in 1949, is still in top shape due to the railroad's attitude toward locomotive appearance and mechanical upkeep. In this yard are engine facilities, general headquarters and shops.

TP&W's one and only GP-30 pounds across the Illinois Central main line (Chicago-New Orleans) at Gilman, Illinois in November of 1970. The engine will not slow down on its westward journey, as the train order hoop is empty. Locomotive was built in 1963 as an EMD 2,250 hp unit, its trucks coming from an F-3 that was traded.

Bound for the East Peoria yard, a 1980 TP&W wayfreight rumbles across the Illinois River, picking up and setting out cars along its route from Effner, Indiana. The big bridge is necessary due to a large barge traffic and the width of the river at this point.

A through freight with three units, with Alco-GE RS-2 #206 leading, comes past the old freight depot at El Paso, Illinois. Maintenance of way machinery on the side track indicates much needed trackwork is being done in this section in 1973.

Union Pacific

Union Pacific 4-8-4 Northern type #828 is being serviced at the engine terminal in Council Bluffs, Iowa. The tender of another 4-8-4, #843, sits alongside in October of 1958.

UP's General Electric gas turbine #61 emits a cloud of black exhaust near the engine facilities at Grand Island, Nebraska in July of 1957. The first test unit (#50), sold the UP on turbines for heavy freight service. A total of 25 units were built from 1953 through 1954.

Alco-GE 1,500 hp FA-1 #1639 leads a westbound freight through Grand Island, Nebraska in the summer of 1957. Locomotive #1639 has piled up thousands of serviceable miles since being built in 1948. What appears to be a flaw in the sky to the right of #1639 is an advertising blimp for a local car dealer.

Looking down from a ladder on the coaling tower at Grand Island, Northern 4-8-4 #825 makes an impressive sight. Although begrimed, it nevertheless is a magnificent machine to behold. However, the cab is no place to be in the 100 plus degree heat on this afternoon in July, 1957.

UP #823, a mighty 4-8-4 Northern, slowly steams ahead with a long string of reefers westbound, its red Mars light, numberboards and main headlight, bell and smoke deflectors all decorating the front end of this massive machine. The freight train is approaching the east yard entrance on the outskirts of Grand Island in July of 1957.

147

Some of UP's good looking power share tracks outside the diesel shop at Omaha in September of 1977. In the center foreground is EMD GP-9 #206, a 1,750 hp unit built in 1954. At right is passenger unit #954, a 2,400 hp E-9 built in 1955.

With the end of regular steam service in sight, #4017 4-8-8-4 leaves Laramie, Wyoming in July of 1957. Locomotive #4017 escaped the wrecking torch by being donated to the National Railroad Museum in Green Bay in 1961.

"Big Blow" GE gas turbine-electric locomotive #63 roars through Rodgers, Nebraska in July of 1957. It was an experience to stand by the tracks when one of these monsters came by: the noise of the turbine was deafening. These powerful 4,500 hp units were capable of high speeds while hauling long trains.

UP hump engines have just released several trailer flats to begin their downward movement to a sorting track at the modern hump yard at North Platte, Nebraska in September of 1977.

Wabash

The Wabash's *Blue Bird* running a little late northbound to Chicago, meets the southbound *Banner Blue* to St. Louis at Decatur. The graceful Alco PA-2 #1052 was built in 1949. The baggageman waits for the train's baggage car to stop opposite his cart. Date: November, 1963.

The switcher is moving cars into Chicago Union Station, including Wabash's solarium-parlor-dome. On a nearby track, GTW steam locomotive #5629 is ready to depart on a fantrip on October of 1966.

St. Louis-bound *Banner Blue* crosses the IC diamond at the entrance to the Decatur, Illinois depot. The leading unit is #638, an EMD F-7A and the trailing unit is #603. The tower at left controls the diamond plus switches in the vicinity.

The Chicago-bound *Blue Bird* crosses the IC diamond at Decatur, Illinois. It's a dreary day, but Alco PA-2 #1052 shows off its handsome design in this profile view taken in November of 1963.

Wabash's *Banner Blue* crosses the Pennsy diamond at Chicago's 21st Street crossing in September of 1951. Power for the St. Louis-bound train is #1003, an EMD E-8A with 2,250 hp.

INDEX

A

Abraham Lincoln, 67-69
Algoma Central, 34,65
Amboy, IL, Depot Museum, 115
Ann Arbor Railroad car ferry, 66,137
Argyle, WI, 83
Argyle & Wooford Flyer, 83
Ashland, WI, 112,133
Aurora, IL, 19

B

Baltimore & Ohio, 10-12,32
Bandana Square, St. Paul, MN, 115
Banner Blue, 150,151
Baraboo, WI, 20,80
Bensenville, IL, 32
"Big Blow," 149
Bluebird (Chicago Great Western), 33
Blue Bird (Wabash), 150,151
Broadway Limited, 4
Bureau Junction, IL, 126
Burlington, WI, 139,140
Burlington Northern, 4,48,113
Butler, WI, 124

C

Calumet, IL, 5,95,97-99
Canadian, 38,39
Canadian National, 5,34-38,52,81
Canadian Pacific, 38-41
Cassleton, ND, 112
Central Station, Chicago, 12,85,87
Central Vermont, 81
Chatsworth, IL, 86
Chenoa, IL, 86
Chesapeake & Ohio, 12,27-31
Chicago, IL, 10-12,25-28,30-32,38,42,58,77,81,
85-87,103,117, 119, 130 137,151
Chicago, Burlington & Quincy, 13-25,87,119
Chicago & Eastern Illinois, 26,27, 77
Chicago & NorthWestern, 4,16, 32,33,70
Chicago & Western Indiana, 4,26,42,59
Chicago, Attica & Southern, 103
Chicago Great Western, 32,33
Chicago River, 68,119
Chicago Short Line, 31,32
Chicago Union Station, 5, 68, 69,117,
120,121,150
Chicago Terminal, 32
Chicago World's Fair, 4
Chief Wawatam, 103,118
City of Miami, 85
City of Milwaukee, 66
City of New Orleans, 4
Clear Lake, IA, 127,130
Cloquet, MN, 48,49,51
Columbus, OH, 104
Corwith Yard, Chicago, 6,7
Council Bluffs, IA, 146
Crescent City, IL, 144

D

Danville Flyer, 26
Dayliner, 40
Dearborn Street Station, 5,7-10, 42,58,
59,77,80, 85
Decatur, IL, 150,151
Detroit Lakes, MN, 74,106,107,114,136
Devil's Lake, ND, 75
Dubuque, IA, 21,23
Duluth, MN, 44,45,52,53,74,113,114,133
Duluth & Northeastern, 48-51
Duluth, Missabe & Iron Range, 43-48,50,54
Duluth, Winnipeg & Pacific, 52,53
Duplainville, WI, 4,132,138
Durand, MI, 5,76,78,80,81

E

Earl Park, IN, 101
East Dubuque, IL, 21,23,24
East Peoria, IL, 144
East St. Louis, IL, 92,143
Effner, IN, 144,145
El Paso, IL, 145

Elgin, Joliet & Eastern, 17,27,54-57, 60,81
Empire Builder, 20
Englewood Station, Chicago, 4, 5, 103
Enola, PA, 117
Eola, IL, 13,17,19
Erie-Lackawanna, 27,57-60,123
Exposition Flyer, 4

F

Fargo, ND, 71,107-109
Fond du Lac, WI, 142
Ft. Francis, Ontario, 52
Ft. Rouge, Winnipeg, 34,36

G

Galena, IL, 84
Galesburg, IL, 19
Gary, IN, 29,101
General Motors, 9
Gilman, IL, 87,145
Golden State, 129
Gopher, 74
Governor's Special, 87
Grand Canyon, 8
Grand Central Station, 5,28
Grand Island, NE, 146,147
Grand Rapids, 79
Grand Trunk Western, 4,5,8,27,30,57-59,
76-81,150
Granville, WI, 139
Great Northern, 71-75,94,112
Greater Winnipeg Water District Railway, 82
Green Bay, WI, 61-66
Green Bay & Western, 61-66
Griffith, IN, 5,27,54,55,57,60,80
Gritty Palace, 65
GTW car ferry, 79
Gulf, Mobile & Ohio, 67-70,105

H

Hammond, IN, 119
Hiawatha, 4,5,11
Hinckley, IL, 21
Hobart, IN, 96
Homby, MN, 48
Horseshoe Curve, Altoona, 122

I

Illinois Central, 4,21,23,32,80,83-87,137
Illinois Central Gulf, 86
Illinois Railway Museum, 115
Illinois River, 145
Indian Bay, Manitoba, 82
Indiana Harbor Belt Railway, 7
Ionia, MI, 77,78
Iowa Terminal, 127
Irwin, IL, 83
Ishpeming, MI, 88

J

James Whitcomb Riley, 103
Joliet, IL, 6,54-56,125,127,130,131
Joliet Union Station, 5,125,128
Jones Island, Milwaukee, 29,79

K

Kentucky Railroad Museum, 95
Kettle Moraine Railway, 33
Kewaunee, WI, 61,63,66
Kewaunee, Green Bay & Western, 61,64
Kilbourn East siding, 134
Kilbourn West siding, 136
Kouts, IN, 123
Kuehler, Otto, 56

L

LaCrosse, WI, 14
Lafayette, IN, 95
Lake Cities, 58,59
Lake Odessa, MI, 30
Lake Shore Limited, 103
Lake Superior & Ishpeming, 88-91
Lake Superior Terminal & Transfer Railway, 53
Laker, 133-135
Lancaster, PA, 123
Land O'Corn, 84

Laramie, WY, 148
LaSalle, IL, 4
LaSalle Street Station, 125,126
Lemont, IL, 67,69,70
Limited, 67-69
Loewy, Raymond, 116
Ludington, MI, 29
Luxemburg, WI, 62

M

Mackinaw City, MI, 103,118
Mainliner, 109,112
Manhattan Limited, 121
McCook, IL,7
Mendota, IL, 86
Mershon Tower, Saginaw, MI, 30
Midday Congressional, 123
Millington, IL, 13,16
Milwaukee, WI, 5,11,20,29,70,141
Milwaukee Electric, 70
Milwaukee Road, 11,132,138,141
Minneapolis, MN, 15,72,74,93,94,106,108,
111,113,133,134
Minneapolis, Northfield & Southern,93,94
Minnesota Railfans Association, 45
Mississippi River, 21,23,24,105,143
Missouri Pacific, 27
Mitchell International Airport, 70
Monon, 95
Morning Zephyr, 21,24
Munising, MI, 91
Museum of Science & Industry, 4
Muskegon, MI, 31,76,78

N

Naperville, IL, 16
National Museum of Transport, 125
National Railroad Historical Society, 24
National Railroad Museum, Green Bay, WI
63,124,148
Nebraska Zephyr, 23
New York Central, 4,68,100-103
Nickel Plate Road, 5,96-99
Nolan, ND, 72,75
Norfolk & Western, 57,100,104,105
North Fond du Lac, WI, 135,138,140
North Lake, WI, 33
North Platte, NE, 149
Northern Pacific, 75,107-114
Northland, 44
Northwestern Steel & Wire, 115

O

Oba, Ontario, 34
Odell, IL, 67
Oelwein, IA, 33
Omaha, NE, 148
Orr, MN, 52
Ottawa, IL, 14,129,131
Ottumwa, IA, 19

P

P.W. Dillon Museum, Sterling, IL, 115
Penn Central, 27,30,77,85,117-119
Pennsylvania Limited, 117,118
Pennsylvania Railroad, 4,7,26,116-123,144
Peoria, IL, 117
Pere Marquette, 30
Pittsburg, PA, 116,118,121
Point Pleasant, NJ, 120
Pontiac, IL, 69
Pontiac, MI, 79
Portage LaPrairie, Manitoba, 37,39,41
Prairie Du Chien, WI, 22
Prairie State, 70
Proctor, MN, 5,43-47
Pullman Junction, IL,32,60,95,104,105,131
Pullman, 44,100

R

Railway Express Agency, 100,133
Rehoboth Beach, DE, 5
Roamer, 63
Robey Street Roundhouse, 10,11
Rochester, MN, 33

Rock Island, IL, 19
Rock Island Railroad, 4,124-131
Rocky Mountain Rocket, 129
Rodgers, NE, 149
Royal Scot, 4

S

Saginaw, MI, 10,30
Saginaw, MN, 48,50
Santa Fe, 4,6-9,11,38,58,59,69,77,80
Sault Ste. Marie, 40
Savanna, IL, 13,14,17,20
Schreiber, Ontario, 38
Seminole, 86
Senator, 122
Sharknose, 116,120
Sheridan, IL, 14
Sheridan, WY, 17
Slinger, WI, 137,141
Soo Line, 4,12,106,107,114,118,132-142
South Bend, IN, 100
South Elgin, IL, 84
Spanish Creek, 11
Spartan, 29
Springfield, IL, 105
St. Boniface, Manitoba, 82
St. Charles, IL, 33
St. Louis, MO, 69,92,100,143
St. Louis Car Company, 9
St. Paul, MN, 25,74,113
Staples, MN, 109
Sterling, IL, 115
Super Chief, 4,8,9
Super Continental, 34
Superior, WI, 71-74,110,112
Sussex, WI, 141,142
Swanington, IN, 103
Sycamore, IL, 32

T

Terminal Railroad Association, 100,143
Terrace Bay, Ontario, 39
Texas Chief, 7
Toledo, Peoria & Western, 86,99,144,145
Transcona, Winnipeg, 35
Trempeleau River Valley Limited, 65
Trenton, NJ, 118
Twentieth Century Limited, 4
Twenty-First Street crossing, Chicago, 5,7,8,
11,26,27,59,68,80, 117,120,151
Twin Cities, MN, 21-24,106

U

Union Depot, Superior, WI, 53
Union Pacific, 146-149

V

Viking, 66,137
Virginia, MN, 44
Vonachan's Junction, IL, 85

W

Wabash Railroad, 150
Washington, IL, 99
Waterloo, IA, 84
Waukegan, IL, 56
Waukesha, WI, 132,134,135,139
Webwood, Ontario, 41
West Hinsdale, IL, 23
Western Maryland Scenic Railroad, 90
Western Pacific, 108
Western Springs, IL, 25
Western Star, 71
Whitcomb Locomotive Company, 13
White River, Ontario, 40
Wilmington, DE, 5,116,122,123
Windsor, Ontario, 5,35,37
Winnipeger, 136
Winona, MN, 33
Wisconsin Dells, WI, 12
Wisconsin Rapids, 65

Z

Zearing, IL, 22
Zephyr, 4